easy knitting
Cosy

easy knitting
Cosy

30 projects to make for your home and to wear

Consultant: Nikki Trench

hamlyn

An Hachette UK Company
www.hachette.co.uk

First published in Great Britain in 2013 by
Hamlyn, a division of Octopus Publishing Group Ltd
Endeavour House
189 Shaftesbury Avenue
London
WC2H 8JY
www.octopusbooks.co.uk

ISBN 978-0-600-62830-9

A CIP catalogue record for this book is available from the
British Library

Printed and bound in China

10 9 8 7 6 5 4 3 2 1

Contents

Introduction 6

Breakfast set 8

Pompom neck wrap 12

Button-through jacket 16

Peruvian-style hat 20

Polka-dot cushion 24

Soft yoga top 28

Snazzy socks 32

Fringed poncho 36

All-stripe gloves 40

Striped scarf with pompoms 44

Felted bobble cushion 48

Soft cape 52

Skinny scarf 56

Fair Isle bobble hat 60

Dotty tea cosy 64

Tea-time treats 68

Cuddly hot-water bottle cover 72

Fair Isle socks 76

Fancy-fringed scarf 80

Striped knitting needle case 84

Boyfriend sweater 88

Featherweight throw 92

Checkered wrap 96

Magazine basket 100

Skinny Fair Isle scarf 104

Aran throw 108

Checked neck wrap 112

Funky Fair Isle tea cosy 116

Repeating flower cushion 120

Cape-style poncho 124

Index 128

Introduction

If you can knit a few basic stitches, you can create stylish knitted items to wear, use to decorate your home and give as gifts for friends and family.

Whether you are a relative beginner, a confident convert or a long-term aficionado, there are projects here to delight. While your first attempts may be a bit uneven, a little practice and experimentation will ensure you soon improve. None of the projects here is beyond the scope of even those fairly new to the hobby.

Knitting is the perfect winter activity, and the finished results can be extremely cosy. Will you make a hot-water bottle cover to snuggle up to, knit one of the scarves and hats or knit something for your home like a tea cosy? Whatever your tastes and experience, there is much to choose from here. All would make charming, unique gifts.

Knitting essentials

All you really need to get knitting is a pair of needles and some yarn. For some projects, that's it; for others additional items are required, most of which can be found in a fairly basic sewing kit. All measurements are given in metric and imperial. Choose which to work in and stick with it since conversions may not be exact.

- **Needles** These come in metric (mm), British and US sizes and are made from different materials, all of which affect the weight and 'feel' of the needles – which you choose is down to personal preference. Circular and double-pointed needles are sometimes used as well.
- **Yarns** Specific yarns are listed for each project, but full details of the yarn's composition and the ball lengths are given so that you can choose alternatives, either from online sources or from your local supplier, many of whom have very knowledgeable staff. Do keep any leftover yarns (not forgetting the ball bands, since these contain vital information) to use for future projects.
- **Additional items**: Some projects require making up and finishing, and need further materials or equipment, such as sewing needles, buttons and other accessories. These are detailed in each project's Getting Started box.

What is in this book

All projects are illustrated with several photographs to show you the detail of the work – both inspirational and useful for reference. A full summary of each project is given in the Getting Started box so you can see exactly what's involved. Here, projects are graded from one ball of yarn (straightforward, suitable for beginners) through two (more challenging) to three balls (for knitters with more confidence and experience).

Also in the Getting Started box is the size of each finished item, yarn(s), needles and additional items needed, and what tension/gauge the project is worked in. Finally, a breakdown of the steps involved is given so you know exactly what the project entails before you start.

At the beginning of the pattern instructions is a key to all abbreviations that are used in that project, while occasional notes expand on the pattern instructions where necessary.

If you have enjoyed the projects here, you may want to explore the other titles in the Easy Knitting series: *Babies & Children*, *Chic*, *Country*, *Vintage & Retro* and *Weekend*. For those who enjoy crochet, a sister series, Easy Crochet, features similarly stylish yet simple projects.

Metric	British	US
2 mm	14	0
2.5 mm	13	1
2.75 mm	12	2
3mm	11	n/a
3.25 mm	10	3
3.5 mm	n/a	4
3.75 mm	9	5
4 mm	8	6
4.5 mm	7	7
5 mm	6	8
5.5 mm	5	9
6 mm	4	10
6.5 mm	3	10.5
7 mm	2	n/a
7.5 mm	1	n/a
8 mm	0	11
9 mm	0	13
10 mm	0	15

Breakfast set

This is a fun knit for a beginner that will cheer up your breakfast table and make a great start to the day.

Brighten up the breakfast table or tray with this combination of tea cosy, placemat and egg cosies knitted in simple garter stitch and classic blue and cream.

The Yarn

Patons Diploma Gold DK is a good-looking and practical mixture of 55% wool, 25% acrylic and 20% nylon. It can be machine washed on a gentle cycle and there are plenty of colours to choose from to coordinate with your own crockery.

GETTING STARTED

New knitters will be encouraged by how easy it is to make this set in basic stitches

Size:

Tea cosy: To fit an average size teapot; width all around approximately 44cm (17½in) and height 16cm (6¼in), excluding pompom

Placemat: 28cm x 38cm (11in x 15in)

Egg cosies: Width all around 17cm (6¾in) and height 8cm (3¼in), excluding pompom

How much yarn:

Patons Diploma Gold DK, approx 120m (131 yards) per ball, in A and B

Tea cosy: 1 ball in each of A and B

Placemat: 2 balls in A and 1 ball in B

Egg cosies (for 2): 1 ball in each of A and B

For complete set: 4 balls in A and 2 balls in B

Needles:

Tea cosy: Pair of 3.25mm (no. 10/US 3) knitting needles

Pair of 3.75mm (no. 9/US 5) knitting needles

Placemat and egg cosies: Pair of 5mm (no. 6/US 8) knitting needles

Tension/gauge:

Tea cosy: 38 sts and 38 rows measure 10cm (4in) square over patt on 3.75mm (no. 9/US 5) needles

Placemat and egg cosies: 17 sts and 32 rows measure 10cm (4in) square over g st with 2 strands of yarn and 5mm (no. 6/US 8) needles

IT IS ESSENTIAL TO WORK TO THE STATED TENSION/GAUGE TO ACHIEVE SUCCESS

What you have to do:

For tea cosy, work throughout in garter stitch with main pattern in two colour vertical stripes forming pleats. Use simple decreasing to shape top of tea cosy within pleat pattern. Decorate top of cosy with a pompom

For placemat, work throughout in garter stitch with stripe pattern at each end. Pick up stitches along both long edges and knit one row to neaten

For egg cosies, work in garter stitch throughout with striped border for one cosy and making bobbles (spots) as instructed for the other. Decorate top of both cosies with small pompoms.

Abbreviations:
cm = centimetre(s); **cont** = continue; **foll** = follows; **g st** = garter stitch (every row knit); **k** = knit; **p** = purl; **patt** = pattern; **psso** = pass slipped stitch over; **rem** = remaining; **rep** = repeat; **RS** = right side; **sl** = slip; **st(s)** = stitch(es); **tog** = together; **WS** = wrong side; **yfwd** = yarn forward/yarn over to make a stitch

Instructions

TEA COSY: (Make 2 pieces alike)
With 3.25mm (no. 10/US 3) needles and A, cast on 88 sts.
K 4 rows.
Change to 3.75mm (no. 9/US 5) needles. Join in B and cont in patt, pulling yarn not in use quite tightly across WS of work to form pleats as foll:
1st row: (RS) K2 B, (6 A, 6 B) to last 2 sts, 2 A.
2nd row: Keeping yarn not in use at back of work, k2 A, (6 B, 6 A) to last 2 sts, 2 B.
Rep these 2 rows to form patt. Patt 44 more rows, ending with a WS row.

Shape top:
1st row: K2 B, (6 A, 2 B, k2tog B, 2 B) to last 2 sts, 2 A. 81 sts.
2nd row: K2 A, (5 B, 6 A) to last 2 sts, 2 B.
3rd row; K2 B, (2 A, k2tog A, 2 A, 5 B) to last 2 sts, 2 A. 74 sts.
4th row: K2 A, (5 B, 5 A) to last 2 sts, 2 B.
5th row: K2 B, (5 A, 1 B, sl 1, k2tog, psso, 1 B) to last 2 sts, 2 A. 60 sts.
6th row: K2 A, (3 B, 5 A) to last 2 sts, 2 B.
7th row: K2 B, (1 A, sl 1, k2tog, psso, 1 A, 3 B) to last 2 sts, 2 A. 46 sts.
8th row: K2 A, (3 B, 3 A) to last 2 sts, 2 B.
9th row: K2 B, (keeping colours as set sl 1, k2tog, psso) to last 2 sts, 2 A. 18 sts.

PLACEMAT: (Use yarn double throughout)
With 5mm (no. 6/US 8) needles and A, cast on 45 sts.
Cont in g st throughout, work (6 rows A and 6 rows B) twice, 74 rows A, (6 rows B and 6 rows A) twice. Cast/bind off with A, but do not cut off yarn.

Edging:
With attached yarn A and RS of work facing, pick up and k62 sts evenly down one long edge of mat (picking up 1 st for every 2 row ends). K 1 row. Cast/bind off.
Work edging in same way along other long edge.

STRIPED EGG COSY: (Use yarn double throughout)
With 5mm (no. 6/US 8) needles and B, cast on 30 sts.
Cont in g st throughout, work 3 rows B, 4 rows A, 4 rows B and 8 rows A.

*Shape top:
Cont in A only.
Next row: (RS) K2, (k2tog, k4) to last 4 sts, k2tog, k2. 25 sts.
Next row: K2, (k2tog, k3) to last 3 sts, k2tog, k1. 20 sts.
Next row: K1, (k2tog, k2) to last 3 sts, k2tog, k1. 15 sts.
Next row: (K1, k2tog) to end. 10 sts.
Next row: (K2tog) to end. 5 sts.
Cut off yarn, thread through rem sts, draw up and fasten off securely.

SPOTTED EGG COSY: (Use yarn double throughout)

With 5mm (no. 6/US 8) needles and A, cast on 30 sts.
Cont in g st throughout, work 3 rows. Cont in patt as foll:

1st row: (RS) K2 A, (make bobble as foll – called MB): join
in B, (k1, yfwd, k1, yfwd, k1) all in next st, turn and k5, turn
and p2tog, p3tog, then pass 2nd st on right needle over 1st
st, leaving 1 st in B on right needle, 9 A) twice, MB, 7 A.

2nd row: With A, k7, (p1, k9) twice, p1, k2.

3rd–6th rows: With A, k to end.

7th row: K7 A, (MB, 9 A) twice, MB, 2 A.

8th row: With A, k2, (p1, k9) twice, p1, k7.

9th–12th rows: With A, k to end.

13th and 14th rows: As 1st and 2nd rows.

With A, k 2 more rows. Complete as given for Striped egg
cosy from * to end.

 ## Making up

TEA COSY:

Join side seams, leaving openings for handle and spout.
With B, make a pompom about 4cm (1½in) in diameter
and sew securely to top of tea cosy.

PLACEMAT:

Sew in ends and neaten corners.

EGG COSIES:

Fold egg cosy in half and join seam. With B, make a pompom
about 3cm (1¼in) in diameter and stitch to top of cosy.

Pompom neck wrap

Ice-cream colours and alternating pompoms make this scarf a fashionable favourite.

This neck wrap is knitted in two coloured halves, so that the contrasting colours appear when it is wrapped around your neck. Knitted in a mixture of cashmere and merino wool it's wonderfully soft and warm.

GETTING STARTED

Quick and easy stocking/stockinette stitch and reverse stocking/stockinette stitch with no shaping

Size:
Wrap is 6.5cm wide x 110cm long (6½in x 43½in)

How much yarn:
2 x 50g (2oz) ball of Debbie Bliss Cashmerino Aran, approx 90m (98 yards) per ball, in colour A
2 balls in colour B

Needles:
Pair of 5mm (no. 6/US 8) needles

Tension/gauge:
18 sts and 24 rows measure 10cm (4in) square over st st on 5mm (no. 6/US 8) needles
IT IS ESSENTIAL TO WORK TO THE STATED TENSION/GAUGE TO ACHIEVE SUCCESS

What you have to do:
Cast on. Work in stocking/stockinette stitch. Change colour. Make pompoms.

The Yarn
Debbie Bliss Cashmerino Aran is a mixture of merino wool, cashmere and microfibre. It is very soft and an excellent weight to work in, particularly for the beginner. Another Aran (fisherman) weight yarn would be a suitable substitute, but look for a yarn that has cashmere added for softness and warmth.

Instructions

Abbreviations:
k = knit; **p** = purl; **st(s)** = stitch(es);
rep = repeat; **cont** = continue

SCARF:
With A, cast on 30 sts.
1st row: K to end.
2nd row: P to end
3rd row: K to end
4th row: P to end
5th row: K to end
6th row: K to end
7th row: P to end
8th row: K to end
9th row: P to end
10th row: K to end
These 10 rows form the ridge pattern and make two ridges.
Work 11 repeats of these 10 rows.
Rep 1st–5th rows.
Change to yarn B. Cont with 6th–10th rows.
Work 12 more repeats of 1st–10th rows.
Cast/bind off knitwise.

HOW TO
CHANGE TO A DIFFERENT COLOURED YARN
This scarf has a change of yarn colour half way through the pattern.

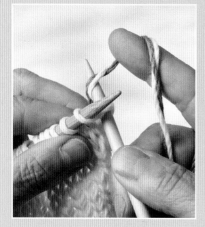

1 Knit in the first colour yarn as instructed. Begin the first row of the new yarn by holding the two types of yarn together in the right hand and knitting the first two stitches with both yarns.

2 Drop the original yarn and continue knitting with the new yarn using just the usual single strand of yarn. Leave the ends of the original yarn at the side of the work, where you can trim them and sew them in later.

HOW TO
MAKE MINI POMPOMS

This scarf is decorated with small pompoms made in alternating colours.

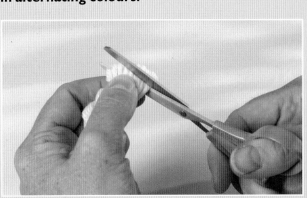

1 Cut a piece of stiff card measuring about 3.5cm (1¼in). The length of the card dictates the size of the finished pompom. Wrap the yarn around the card about 20 times.

3 Cut the ends of the loops to make the pompom and trim so that they are the same length all round.

2 Slide the yarn off the card and tie a piece of yarn tightly around the middle of the loops of yarn. Tie in a double knot.

4 Fluff the pompom into shape with your fingers. Leave the yarn tied around the middle and use this to attach the pompom.

 Making up

Sew in all the loose ends of yarn by threading them onto a large yarn needle and taking them under several stitches, then trim off the excess yarn.

Making the mini pompoms:
Make 7 pink and 7 cream mini pompoms as described above.
Thread the yarn that has been used to tie the middle of the pompoms onto a large yarn needle. Sew the pompoms onto the cast on and cast/bound-off edges of the scarf, alternating the colours. Secure the ends and trim off excess yarn on each pompom.

Button-through jacket

This classic jacket is cosy but light, so it's perfect for sunny days when there's still a chill in the air.

No wardrobe should be without this classic jacket for casual wear. It is knitted in Aran (fisherman) yarn and moss/seed stitch throughout, with a collar and set-in pockets.

The Yarn

Debbie Bliss Cashmerino Aran is 100% merino wool in a weight that is ideal for outer garments and a crisp finish that enhances stitch patterns, such as moss/seed stitch. It is available in traditional, neutral Aran shades, or beautiful bright colours for a more contemporary look.

GETTING STARTED

Easy moss/seed-stitch fabric but take care to knit evenly for the best appearance

Size:
To fit bust: 81–86[91–97:102–107]cm/ 32–34[36–38:40–42]in
Actual size: 97.5[110:119]cm/38½[43½:47]in
Length from shoulder: 60[62:64]cm/ 23¾[24½:25¼]in
Sleeve seam: 41[43:45]cm/16[17:17¾]in
Note: Figures in square brackets [ ] refer to larger sizes; where there is only one set of figures, it applies to all sizes

How much yarn:
16[17:19] x 50g (2oz) balls of Debbie Bliss Cashmerino Aran, approx 90m (98 yards) per ball

Needles:
Pair of 5mm (no. 6/US 8) knitting needles

Additional items:
4 buttons
Stitch holders

Tension/gauge:
17 sts and 30 rows measure 10cm (4in) square over moss/seed st on 5mm (no. 6/US 8) needles
IT IS ESSENTIAL TO WORK TO THE STATED TENSION/GAUGE TO ACHIEVE SUCCESS

What you have to do:
Work in moss/seed stitch. Work simple decreasing and increasing to shape sides, armholes and front neck edges. Make set-in pockets with separate linings. Make separate collar and sew to neck edge.

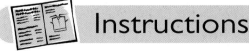 Instructions

Abbreviations:

alt = alternate; **beg** = beginning; **cm** = centimetre(s); **cont** = continue; **dec** = decrease(ing); **foll** = following; **inc** = increase(ing); **k** = knit; **p** = purl; **patt** = pattern; **rem** = remaining; **RS** = right side; **st(s)** = stitch(es); **tog** = together; **WS** = wrong side; **yfwd** = yarn forward/yarn over

BACK:

Cast on 81[91:99] sts. Cont in patt as foll:

1st row: (RS) K1, (p1, k1) to end.

2nd row: As 1st row.

These 2 rows form moss/seed st patt. Work more 8 rows in patt.

Keeping patt correct, dec 1 st at each end of next and every foll 8th row to 73[83:91] sts. Work 13 rows straight, then inc 1 st at each end of next and every foll 12th row to 81[91:99] sts. Cont straight until Back measures 38cm (15in) from beg, ending with a WS row.

Shape armholes:

Cast/bind off 4 sts at beg of next 2 rows. Dec 1 st at each end of every row to 65[71:75] sts, then at each end of every foll alt row to 57[61:65] sts. Cont straight until armholes measure 20[22:24]cm/8[8¾:9½]in, ending with a WS row.

Shape shoulders and back neck:

Cast/bind off 5 sts at beg of next 2 rows. 47[51:55] sts.

Next row: Cast/bind off 5 sts, patt until there are 14[15:16] sts on right needle, turn and leave rem sts on a spare needle.

Next row: Cast/bind off 5 sts, patt to end.

Next row: Cast/bind off 4[5:6] sts, patt to end.

Cast/bind off rem 5 sts. With RS facing, rejoin yarn to rem sts, Cast/bind off centre 9[11:13] sts evenly in patt, patt to end.

Next row: Cast/bind off 5 sts, patt to end.

Complete to match first side, reversing shapings.

POCKET LININGS: (Make 2)

Cast on 21 sts. Work in moss/seed st for 12cm (4¾in). Cut off yarn and leave sts on a holder.

LEFT FRONT:

Cast on 45[51:55] sts. Work 10 rows in moss/seed st, ending with a WS row. Dec 1 st at beg of next and every foll 8th row to 41[47:51] sts. Work 2 rows straight, ending with a RS row.

Place pocket lining:

Next row: Patt 12[14:16] sts, Cast/bind off next 21 sts evenly in patt, patt to end.

Next row: Patt 8[12:14] sts, patt across 21 sts from first pocket lining, patt to end. 41[47:51] sts.

Work 9 rows straight, then inc 1 st at beg of next and every foll 12th row to 45[51:55] sts. Cont straight until Front matches Back to start of armhole shaping, ending with a WS row.

Shape armhole:

Next row: Cast/bind off 4 sts, patt to end.

Work 1 row straight. Dec 1 st at armhole edge on next 4[6:8] rows, then on every foll alt row to 33[36:38] sts. Cont straight until Front measures 5[5:6]cm/2[2:2½]in less than Back to start of shoulder shaping, ending with a RS row.

Shape neck:

Cast/bind off 5[5:6] sts at beg of next row and 4 sts at beg of 2[3:3] foll alt rows. 20[19:20] sts. Work 1 row. Cast/bind off 2 sts at beg of next and 2[1:1] foll alt rows. 14[15:16] sts. Work a few rows straight until Front matches Back to shoulder, ending with a WS row.

Shape shoulder:

Cast/bind off 5 sts at beg of next and foll alt row. Cast/bind off rem 4[5:6] sts.

RIGHT FRONT:

Work as for Left front, reversing shapings and making 4 buttonholes – the first to come 16cm (6¼in) from lower edge and last 4 rows from neck edge, with the remainder spaced evenly between.

Buttonhole row: (RS) Patt 3 sts, yfwd, k2tog, patt to end. Note also that row 'place pocket lining' will read as foll:

Next row: Patt 8[12:14] sts, Cast/bind off 21 sts evenly in patt, patt to end.

Next row: Patt 12[14:16] sts, patt across 21 sts from second pocket lining, patt to end. 41[47:51] sts.

SLEEVES: (Make 2)

With 5mm (no. 6/US 8) needles cast on 39[43:45] sts.

Cont in moss/seed st, inc 1 st at each end of 9th and every foll 12th[16th:14th] row to 47[57:55] sts.

1st and 3rd sizes only:

Inc 1 st at each end of every foll 14th[16th] row to 55[61] sts.

All sizes:

55[57:61] sts. Work straight until sleeve measures 41[43:45]cm/16[17:17¾]in from beg, ending with a WS row.

Shape top:

Cast/bind off 4 sts at beg of next 2 rows. 47[49:53] sts. Dec 1 st at each end of next and every foll 4th row to 29[27:29] sts, then at each end of every foll alt row to 23 sts. Dec 1 st at each end of every row until 17 sts rem. Cast/bind off evenly in patt.

COLLAR:

Join shoulder seams.

Cast on 71[79:87] sts. Work in moss/seed st for 8cm (3¼in).

Shape collar:

Cast/bind off 6[6:7] sts at beg of next 8 rows. Cast/bind off rem 23[31:31] sts.

Placing shaped edge of collar to cast/bound-off edge of neck, sew in position easing to fit and leaving a slight gap at centre front to allow for overlap (of about 3 sts).

Making up

Do not press.
Slip stitch pocket linings in place on WS of work.
Sew in sleeves. Join side and sleeve seams.
Sew on buttons.

Peruvian-style hat

With striped ear flaps and a patterned crown, this cosy hat echoes a traditional Peruvian design.

Worked in natural colouring and simple colour patterns, this snug pull-on hat has typical Peruvian styling with a tassel trim, ear flaps and cord ties.

The Yarn

The pure wool content and graded natural colourings of Peruvian-style designs can easily be sourced from the Mode DK range by Wendy. In addition, a project knitted in this yarn can be machine washed on a wool cycle and even tumble-dried on a low setting.

GETTING STARTED

The fabric is stocking/stockinette stitch but colourwork includes simple stripe and intarsia patterns with yarn carried across the back of the work

Size:
One size to fit average size woman's head
Width around head: *55cm (21½in)*

How much yarn:
1 x 50g (2oz) ball of Wendy Mode DK Pure New Wool, approx 142m (155 yards) per ball, in each of four colours A, B, C and D

Needles:
Pair of 3.75mm (no. 9/US 5) knitting needles
Pair of 4mm (no. 8/US 6) knitting needles
Pair of 4.5mm (no. 7/US 7) knitting needles
Spare 3.75mm (no. 9/US 5) knitting needle

Tension/gauge:
22 sts and 30 rows measure 10 cm (4in) square over st st on 4mm (no. 8/US 6) needles
IT IS ESSENTIAL TO WORK TO THE STATED TENSION/GAUGE TO ACHIEVE SUCCESS

What you have to do:
Work in stocking/stockinette stitch and garter stitch. Shape work with invisible increases (making a stitch) and working two stitches together to decrease. Work stripes. Pick up stitches and work edgings. Work colour patterns, carrying yarn not in use across back of work. Make twisted cords.

Instructions

Abbreviations:

alt = alternate; **beg** = beginning; **cont** =continue; **dec** = decrease(ing); **foll** = following; **g st** = garter stitch (every row k); **k** = knit; **m l k** = make a stitch by picking up horizontal loop lying before next stitch and knitting into back of it; **m l p** = make a stitch by picking up horizontal loop lying before next stitch and purling into back of it; **p** = purl; **patt** = pattern; **rem** = remain(ing); **rep** = repeat; **RS** = right side; **st(s)** = stitch(es); **st st** = stocking/stockinette stitch; **tog** = together; **WS** = wrong side

Note: When working 3rd–8th , 11th–14th and 21st and 22nd rows of pattern on Hat, strand yarn not in use loosely across WS of work over not more than 3 sts at a time to keep fabric elastic.

EAR FLAPS: (Make 2)

With 4mm (no. 8/US 6) needles and A, cast on 3 sts.
1st row: (RS) K to end.
2nd row: P1, m l p, p1, m l p, p1. 5 sts.
3rd row: K1, m l k, k3, m l k, k1. 7 sts.
4th row: P to end. Cut off A and join in B.
5th row: With B, k1, m l k, k to last st, m l k, k1.
6th row: P to end.
7th row: As 5th row. 11 sts. Cut off B and join in C.
8th row: With C, p to end.
9th row: With C, as 5th row. 13 sts.
10th row: P to end. Cut off C and join in A.
11th row: With A, as 5th row. 15 sts.
12th row: P to end.
13th row: As 11th row. 17 sts. Cut off A and join in B.
14th row: With B, p to end.
15th row: As 5th row. 19 sts.

16th row: P to end. Cut off B and join in C.

17th row: With C, k to end.

18th row: With C, p1, m1p, p to last st, m1p, p1. 21 sts.

19th row: K to end. Cut off C and join in A.

20th–22nd rows: As 14th–16th rows, but using A instead of B. 23 sts. Cut off A and join in B.

23rd–25th rows: As 17th–19th rows, but using B instead of C. 25 sts. Cut off B and join in C.

26th–28th rows: As 14th–16th rows, but using C instead of B. 27 sts. Joining in and cutting off colours as required and beg with a k row, cont in st st and stripes as foll: Work 3 rows each in A, B, C and A, ending with a WS row. Cast/bind off.

Left side edging:

With 3.75mm (no. 9/US 5) needles, D and RS facing, beg at cast/bound-off edge of left side of first Ear Flap and pick up and k35 sts along shaped row-ends to centre of cast-on edge. Cast/bind off knitways.

Right side edging:

With 3.75mm (no. 9/US 5) needles, D and RS facing, beg at centre of cast-on edge of first Ear Flap and pick up and k35 sts along right side of shaped row-ends to cast/bound-off edge. Cast/bind off knitways.

Top edging:

With 3.75mm (no. 9/US 5) needles, D and RS facing, pick up and k27 sts across cast/bound-off edge of first Ear Flap.

K1 row. Cut off yarn and leave these sts on a holder. Work Left side edging, Right side edging and Top edging in same way on second Ear Flap.

HAT:

With spare 3.75mm (no. 9/US 5) needle and D, cast on 14 sts, cut off yarn, then on same needle and with D, cast on 39 sts, cut off yarn. With 3.75mm (no. 9/US 5) needles and D, cast on 14 sts, k these 14 sts, with RS facing, k across 27 sts of first Ear Flap, k39 sts from spare needle, k across 27 sts of second Ear Flap, then k14 sts from spare needle.

121 sts. Work in 5 rows in g st, ending with a WS row. Cut off D. Change to 4mm (no. 8/US 6) needles. Joining in and cutting off colours as required, cont in patt as foll:

1st row: (RS) With B, k to end.

2nd row: With B, p to end.

Change to 4.5mm (no. 7/US 7) needles.

3rd row: K1 C, * 6 A, 2 C, rep from * to end.

4th row: *P3 C, 5 A, rep from * to last st, 1 C.

5th row: K1 C, *4 A, 4 C, rep from * to end.

6th row: P3 C, *2 C, 6 A, rep from * to last 6 sts, 2 C, 4 A.

7th row: K3 C, *3 C, 5A, rep from * to last 6 sts, 3 C, 3 A.

8th row: P3 A, *4 C, 4 A, rep from * to last 6 sts, 4 C, 2 A.

Change to 4mm (no. 8/US 6) needles.

9th row: With D, k to end.

10th row: With D, p to end.

Change to 4.5mm (no. 7/US 7) needles.

11th row: K4 B, *1 C, 7 B, rep from * to last 5 sts, 1 C, 4 B.

12th row: P3 B, *3 C, 5 B, rep from * to last 6 sts, 3 C, 3 B.

13th row: K2 B, *5 C, 3 B, rep from * to last 7 sts, 5 C, 2 B.

14th row: P1 B, *7 C, 1 B, rep from * to end.

Change to 4mm (no. 8/US 6) needles.

15th–18th rows: With A, work 4 rows in st st.

19th row: With D, k to end.

20th row: With D, p19, p2tog, (p38, p2tog) twice, p20. 118 sts. Change to 4.5mm (no. 7/US 7) needles.

21st row: K2 B, *2 D, 2 B, rep from * to end.

22nd row: P2 B, *2 D, 2 B, rep from * to end.

Change to 4mm (no. 8/US 6) needles.

23rd –24th rows: With C, work 2 rows in st st.

25th row: With A, k to end.

26th row: With A, p6, p2tog, (p11, p2tog) 8 times, p6. 109 sts.

27th–28th rows: With D, work 2 rows in st st.

Shape crown:

1st row: (RS) With B, k to end.

2nd row: With B, p1, (p2tog, p7) 12 times. 97 sts.

3rd row: With C, k to end.

4th row: With C, p1, (p2tog, p6) 12 times. 85 sts.

5th row: With A, k to end.

6th row: With A, p1, (p2tog, p5) 12 times. 73 sts.

Cont in this way, dec 12 sts on every foll alt row, until 25 sts rem and working in stripes of 2 rows each A, D, B and C.

15th row: With C, (k2tog) 12 times, k1. 13 sts.

Cut off yarn, thread through rem sts, pull up tightly and fasten off securely.

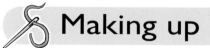

Making up

Press carefully, following instructions on ball band. Join back seam.

Using 4 strands of D, make 2 twisted cords 25cm (10in) long and attach one to pointed end of each Ear Flap.

Using 4 strands of D, make a twisted cord 8cm (3in) long. Using D, make a tassel 10cm (4in) long and attach to end of twisted cord. Thread other end of twisted cord through top of hat and sew securely in place.

HOW TO
MAKE A TASSEL

Tassels can be used to decorate all kinds of knitted items – but remember they use a lot of yarn.

I Decide on the length of tassel you want and then cut a piece of stiff card to the same dimension. Wrap the yarn around the card until you have approximately the right quantity for the finished tassel. Cut off the yarn at the end of the cardboard.

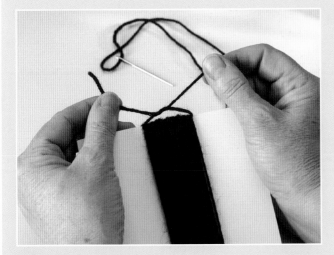

2 Thread another piece of yarn onto a blunt-ended needle and pass the needle under the yarn at the top of the card. Tie the yarn in a knot, leaving a long length of yarn.

3 Cut along the yarn at the bottom edge of the cardboard and remove the cardboard. Push the needle threaded with the length of yarn down into the centre of the tassel from the top.

4 Bring the needle out of the tassel and wrap the yarn around the tassel about 4.5cm (1½in) from the top. Continue wrapping until you have created a band of yarn around the tassel.

5 Thread the needle through the top of the tassel and trim the yarn, leaving enough to attach the tassel. Trim the bottom edges of the tassel to ensure they are even.

Polka-dot cushion

Make a graphic statement to match your decor with this bright and funky cushion/pillow.

This eye-catching design has bold, white polka dots against a blue back-ground. Knitted in stocking/stockinette stitch, the back has a buttoned opening.

The Yarn
Patons Diploma Gold DK is a mixture of wool and man-made fibres that is perfect for home furnishings as it is hard wearing. It can also be machine washed on a wool cycle. There is also a large colour range with plenty of strong colours that make good backgrounds for white polka dots.

GETTING STARTED

 The fabric is simple stocking/stockinette stitch but the spots are worked from a chart using the intarsia technique

Size:
Cushion/pillow is 41cm (16in) square

How much yarn:
4 x 50g (2oz) balls of Patons Diploma Gold DK, approx 120m (131 yards) per ball, in colour A
1 ball in colour B

Needles:
Pair of 4mm (no. 8/US 6) knitting needles

Additional items:
3 flat white buttons, 4cm (1½in) in diameter
41cm (16in) square cushion pad/pillow form

Tension/gauge:
22 sts and 30 rows measure 10cm (4in) square over st st using 4mm (no. 8/US 6) needles
IT IS ESSENTIAL TO WORK TO THE STATED TENSION/ GAUGE TO ACHIEVE SUCCESS

What you have to do:
Work in stocking/stockinette stitch. Read chart to work pattern. Use intarsia technique of colour knitting to work with several small balls of yarn across a row. Cast/bind off and cast on stitches to make a buttonhole.

Instructions

Abbreviations:
beg = beginning; **cont** = continue(ing);
cm = centimetre(s); **k** = knit; **p** = purl; **patt** = pattern;
RS = right side; **rep** = repeat; **st(s)** = stitch(es);
st st = stocking/stockinette stitch; **WS** = wrong side

CUSHION/PILLOW:
With A, cast on 90 sts and commence at lower back.
1st row: (RS) K2, *p2, k2, rep from * to end.
2nd row: P2, *k2, p2, rep from * to end.

Beg with a k row, cont in st st and work 100 rows.
Front:
Cont in st st and patt from chart. Read odd-numbered (RS) rows from right to left and even-numbered (WS) rows from left to right. Use a separate small ball for each area of colour, twisting yarns together on WS of work when changing colour to avoid a hole forming.
1st row: K9 A, work 1st row of chart, k9 A.
2nd row: P9 A, work 2nd row of chart, p9 A.
These 2 rows set position of chart and edge sts in

st st and A. Cont as set, work 40 rows of chart 3 times – 120 rows in all.

Upper back:

Cont in A only and work 48 rows in st st.

1st buttonhole row: K20, cast/bind off 4 sts, (k19 including st used to cast/bind off, cast/bind off 4 sts) twice, k to end.

2nd buttonhole row: P to end, casting on 4 sts over those cast/bound off on previous row. Rep 1st and 2nd rib rows as given for lower back. Cast/bind off in rib.

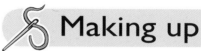

Making up

Neatly sew in all loose ends on WS of cushion/pillow front. Press carefully on RS of work, using a cool iron over a dry cloth. Fold cushion/pillow to form a square so that the upper back section overlaps lower back section. Slipstitch overlapped section together along side edges. With RS together backstitch side seams. Turn cover to RS through opening. Sew on buttons to correspond with buttonholes. Insert cushion pad/pillow form.

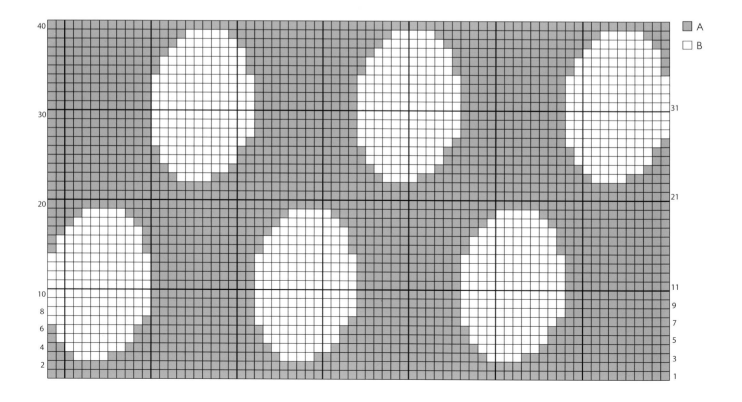

HOW TO
WORK IN COLOUR

The intarsia method is a way of knitting blocks of colour within a knitted fabric. A separate length of yarn is kept for each different colour and the yarns are twisted together where the colours change to make a single piece of fabric without holes between the colours.

1 Instead of having a whole ball of yarn attached to each block of colour you can wind a smaller amount of yarn around a bobbin, or make a smaller ball. Plastic bobbins are available from most knitting suppliers: you simply wrap the yarn around them working from the cut end of the yarn towards the end attached to the knitting. If you want to wind your own smaller balls, start by spreading out the finger and thumb of one hand and wrapping the yarn around them in a figure-of-eight. Remove the yarn from your fingers, keeping the shape, and then wrap the remaining yarn around the middle of the figure-of-eight. Pull the loose end from the centre of the yarn and work from this.

2 When you change to a new colour you need to twist the yarns together at the back of the work. To do this, place the new yarn over the working yarn and then wrap the new yarn around the working yarn. Pick up the new yarn and release the working yarn and continue the next stitch with the new yarn. Wrapping the new yarn around the working yarn in this way joins the two colours together vertically and stops a gap forming between the two colours.

Soft yoga top

Chill out in this soft, loose, hooded top that is easy to knit and relaxing to wear.

Worked in stocking/stockinette stitch with garter-stitch edgings, this simple top combines style with comfort.

GETTING STARTED

Simple shaping and pattern stitches but care is needed to pick up stitches evenly around the neck

Size:

To fit bust: 81–86[86–91:97–102]cm/ 32–34[34–36:38–40]in

Actual size: 97.5[104:113]cm/38½[41:44½]in

Length: 62[64:66]cm/23¾[24½:25¼]in

Sleeve seam: 40cm (15¾in)

Note: Figures in square brackets [ ] refer to larger sizes; where there is only one set of figures, it applies to all sizes

How much yarn:

14[15:16] x 50g (2oz) balls of Debbie Bliss Cashmerino Aran, approx 90m (98 yards) per ball

Needles:

Pair of 5mm (no. 6/US 8) knitting needles
5mm (no. 6/US 8) circular knitting needle

Additional items:

Stitch holder, stitch marker

Tension/gauge:

18 sts and 24 rows measure 10cm (4in) square over st st on 5mm (no. 6/US 8) needles
IT IS ESSENTIAL TO WORK TO THE STATED TENSION/GAUGE TO ACHIEVE SUCCESS

What you have to do:

Work in stocking/stockinette stitch with garter-stitch edge on side opening, neck opening and hood edges. Work decorative paired shapings on the raglan armholes. Pick up stitches around the neck to work the hood.

The Yarn

Containing a mixture of 55% merino wool with 33% microfibre and 12% cashmere, Debbie Bliss Cashmerino Aran is a luxurious yarn with a slight sheen. Its silky-soft handle is perfect for warmth and comfort, and there is a wide colour palette to choose from, with plenty of subtle fashion shades.

Abbreviations:

alt = alternate;
beg = beginning;
cm = centimetre(s);
cont = continue;
dec = decrease(ing);
foll = follow(s)(ing);
inc = increase(ing);
k = knit;
m1 = make 1 stitch by picking up horizontal loop between needles and working into back of it;
p = purl; **patt** = pattern;
rem = remain(ing);
rep = repeat;
RS = right side;
st(s) = stitch(es);
st st = stocking/stockinette stitch;
tbl = through back of loops; **tog** = together;
WS = wrong side

Instructions

BACK:

With 5mm (no. 6/US 8) needles cast on 88[94:102] sts. K3 rows.

Next row: (RS) K to end.

Next row: K3, p to last 3 sts, k3.

Rep last 2 rows until Back measures 9cm (3½in), ending with a WS row.

Beg with a k row, cont in st st until Back measures 37cm (14½in) from beg, ending with a WS row.

Shape raglan armholes:

Cast/bind off 4 sts at beg of next 2 rows. 80[86:94] sts.

3rd row: K2, k2tog, k to last 4 sts, k2tog tbl, k2.

4th row: P to end.

5th row: K to end.

6th row: P to end.

Rep 3rd–6th rows until 74[78:84] sts rem, then 3rd and 4th rows only until 28[32:36] sts rem. Cast/bind off.

FRONT:

Work as given for Back until 58[64:70] sts rem when shaping raglan armholes, ending with a WS row.

Divide for neck opening:

Next row: K2, k2tog, k25[28:31], turn and leave rem sts on a spare needle. 28[31:34] sts.

Complete this side of neck first.

Next row: K3, p to end.

Next row: K2, k2tog, k to end.

Rep last 2 rows until 14[16:18] sts rem, ending with a WS row. Cut off yarn and leave sts on a holder.

With RS of work facing, rejoin yarn to rem sts, k to last 4 sts, k2tog tbl, k2.

Next row: P to last 3 sts, k3.

Complete to match first side of neck, ending with a WS row, but do not cut off yarn (this will be used for working the hood).

SLEEVES: (Make 2)

With 5mm (no. 6/US 8) needles cast on 46[50:56] sts. K 3 rows. Beg with a k row, cont in st st, inc one st (2 sts in from edge) at each end of 5th and every foll 6th row until there are 68[72:78] sts. Inc one st at each end of every foll 8th row twice. 72[76:82] sts. Work straight until Sleeve measures 40cm (15¾in) from beg, ending with a WS row.

Shape top:

Cast/bind off 4 sts at beg of next 2 rows. 64[68:74] sts. Rep 3rd–6th rows of Back raglan shaping until 56[60:66] sts rem, then rep 3rd and 4th rows only until 14 sts rem, ending with a WS row. Cast/bind off.

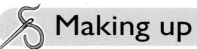 Making up

PRESSING:
Following instructions given on ball band, press very lightly on WS, avoiding garter-stitch edges.
Join raglan seams, using backstitch.

HOOD:
With 5mm (no. 6/US 8) circular needle and RS of work facing, return to ball of yarn attached at right front neck and work as foll: k14[16:18] sts from right front neck, pick up and k14 sts from right sleeve, 27[31:35] sts from back neck, 14 sts from left sleeve, then k across 14[16:18] sts from left front neck. 83[91:99] sts. Place a marker on st at centre back neck.
Next row: K3, p to last 3 sts, k3.
Work 2 more rows in st st and edge patt as set.
Shape back of hood:
Increase row: (RS) K to marked st, m1, k marked st, m1, k to end. Work 3 more rows in st st and edge patt as set.
Rep last 4 rows 3 times more, then work inc row again. 93[101:109] sts. Work straight in patt until hood measures 28[29:30]cm/11[11½:11¾]in, ending with a WS row.
Shape top:
Next row: K to within 2 sts of marked st, k2tog, k marked st, k2tog tbl, k to end.
Work 3 rows in st st and patt as set.
Next row: K to within 2 sts of marked st, k2tog, k marked st, k2tog tbl, k to end.
Cont to dec in this way on every foll alt row to 83[91:99] sts, ending with a RS row. Cast/bind off.
Join hood seam. Join sleeve seams and side seams to top of side opening.

Snazzy socks

Perfect for lounging around in when it's too chilly for bare feet, these socks are soft and snuggly.

Relax and keep warm in these funky, chunky socks in brightly coloured variegated yarn with ribbed tops and edged with a solid-coloured frill. The heels and toes are knitted in a toning solid colour.

The Yarn

King Cole Magnum Chunky is a mixture of 75% hard-wearing acrylic with 25% wool, making it soft, thick but lightweight. The Multi shades are variegated in a fun range of bright colours to give a tweed effect. They can easily be teamed with the plain colours in the Magnum range.

GETTING STARTED

The stocking/stockinette fabric with ridges is easy but working in rounds with four double-pointed needles is a skill that needs practice

Size:

To fit small: *[medium: large] woman's foot*

Actual size, heel to toe: *24[26:28]cm/19½[10¼:11]in*

Top edge to back heel: *18[19:20]cm/7[7½:8]in*

Note: *Figures in square brackets [ ] refer to larger sizes; where there is only one set of figures, it applies to all sizes*

How much yarn:

1 x 100g (3½oz) ball of King Cole Magnum Multi Chunky, approx 110m (120 yards) per ball, in main colour A

1 x 100g (3½oz) ball of King Cole Magnum Chunky, approx 110m (120 yards) per ball, in contrast colour B

Needles:

Set of 5mm (no. 6/US 8) double-pointed knitting needles

Set of 6mm (no. 4/US 10) double-pointed knitting needles

Pair of 5mm (no. 6/US 8) knitting needles

Tension/gauge:

14 sts and 21 rows measure 10cm (4in) square over st st on 6mm (no. 4/US 10) needles

IT IS ESSENTIAL TO WORK TO THE STATED TENSION/ GAUGE TO ACHIEVE SUCCESS

What you have to do:

Cast on with a pair of needles and work frilled edging. Divide stitches on to set of four double-pointed needles and work in rounds. Shape heel, gusset and toe as directed in instructions.

Instructions

Abbreviations:

beg = beginning; **cm** = centimetre(s); **cont** = continue; **foll** = follow(s)(ing); **k** = knit; **p** = purl; **patt** = pattern; **psso** = pass slipped stitch over; **rem** = remain(ing); **rep** = repeat; **RS** = right side; **sl** = slip; **st(s)** = stitch(es); **st st** = stocking/stockinette stitch; **tbl** = through back of loop; **tog** = together; **yfwd** = yarn forward/yarn over; **yon** = yarn over needle

SOCKS:

With pair of 5mm (no. 6/US 8) needles and B, cast on 42[52:62] sts. Work edging in rows as foll:

1st row: (RS) K1, yfwd, *k5, sl successively 2nd, 3rd, 4th and 5th sts just worked over 1st and off needle, yfwd, rep from * to last st, k1. 19[23:27] sts.

2nd row: P1, *p1, yon, k1 tbl, rep from * to end. 28[34:40] sts.

Change to set of 5mm (no. 6/US 8) double-pointed needles and A and divide sts on to four needles as foll:

1st and 3rd sizes only:

7[10] sts on needles 1, 2, 3 and 4. 28[40] sts. Join, taking care not to twist sts on needle.

2nd size only:

8 sts on needles 1 and 4, 9 sts on needles 2 and 3, dec 1 st in centre of needles 2 and 3. 32 sts. Join, taking care not to twist sts on needle.

All sizes:

Place a marker between needles 1 and 4 to denote beg of round and centre back.

1st round: K to end.

2nd round: *K2, p2, rep from * to end. Rep 2nd round until work measures 5cm (2in) from beg of rib in A.

Change to set of 6mm (no. 4/US 10) needles. Cont in A and main patt as foll: K4 rounds and then P1 round. Rep last 5 rounds twice more. Cut off yarn.

Heel:

With B, k14[16:20] sts from needles 4 and 1, leaving rem 14[16:20] sts on needles 2 and 3.

With B, work back and forth in st st for 9[11:13] rows.

Turn heel:

Next row: (RS) K9[10:13], sl 1, k1, psso, turn.

Next row: Sl 1, p4[4:6], sl 1, p1, psso, turn.

Next row: Sl 1, k4[4:6], sl 1, k1, psso, turn.

Rep last 2 rows until all sts have been worked from these needles. Cut off yarn and leave these 6[6:8] sts on a

spare needle.

With A and RS facing, pick up and k7[9:11] sts along heel edge, k across 6[6:8] sts from needle, then pick up and k 7[9:11] sts along other side of heel. 20[24:30] sts. Divide these sts between needles 1 and 4, then work over sts on needles 2 and 3 to end at centre sole. 34 [40:50] sts.

Gusset:

1st round: K to last st on needle 1, k tog last st from needle 1 and 1st st from needle 2, k to last st on needle 3, sl 1, k1, psso from last st on needle 3 and 1st st on needle 4, k to end of round.

2nd round: K to last 2 sts on needle 1, k2tog, k12[14:18] sts on needles 2 and 3, on needle 4, sl 1, k1, psso. K to end of round. Rep 2nd round until 28[32:40] sts rem, ending at centre sole.

Re-arrange sts so that 7[8:10] sts are on each needle. Cont in patt as foll:

4th round: K7[8:10] sts from needle 1, p14[16:20] sts from needles 2 and 3, k7[810] sts from needle 4.

5th, 6th, 7th and 8th rounds: K to end.

Rep last 4 rounds until required length for foot is worked, allowing 5[6:7]cm/2[2½:2¾]in for toe. Cut off yarn.

Shape toe:

With B, k 2 rounds.

Next round: K to last 2 sts on needle 1, k2tog, sl 1, k1,

psso, on needle 2, k to last 2 sts on needle 3, k2tog, sl 1,
k1, psso, on needle 4, k to end of round.
Next round: K to end.
Rep last 2 rounds until 8[8:12] sts rem. Cut off yarn,
leaving a long end. Thread a double strand of yarn
through rem sts, draw up and fasten off securely.

Fringed poncho

This poncho is the perfect garment to slip on over a pair of jeans to keep chilly winds at bay.

Knitted in chunky yarn, this trendy poncho will quickly grow before your eyes. It looks great with everything from jeans to summer dresses.

GETTING STARTED

Some increasing and shaping plus eyelet holes for pattern above fringing, but most of the poncho is straightforward

Size:
Length: 50cm (20in), excluding fringe
Width (at lower edge): 250cm (98½in)

How much yarn:
6 x 100g (3½oz) balls of Sirdar Denim Chunky, approx 156m (171 yards) per ball

Needles:
Pair of 6.5mm (no. 3/US 10½) knitting needles
Short 6.5mm (no. 3/US 10½) circular needle

Additional items:
Crochet hook for fringing

Tension/gauge:
14 stitches and 19 rows to 10cm (4in) in stocking/ stockinette stitch; 13 stitches to 10cm (4in) and 8 rows measure 5cm (2in) over eyelet pattern, all on 6.5mm (no. 3/US 10½) needles
IT IS ESSENTIAL TO WORK TO THE STATED TENSION/ GAUGE TO ACHIEVE SUCCESS

What you have to do:
Cast on. Work in stocking/stockinette stitch (st st). Increase stitches to shape panels. Make stitches to form eyelet holes. Cast/bind off. Knit collar on circular needle (optional). Make fringing.
Note: The poncho is knitted in four sections, and the collar is worked in the round after the sections have been joined. See page 39 if you prefer to work the collar on two needles.

The Yarn
Sirdar Denim Chunky is a range in which most of the colours are blended so they have a denim appearance. A mix of 60% acrylic, 25% cotton and 15% wool gives it a lovely soft feel.

Abbreviations:

beg = beginning;
cont = continue;
foll = following;
inc = increase; **k** = knit;
kfb = k into front and back of st;
patt = pattern;
p = purl;
pfb = purl into front and back of st;
RS = right side;
st(s) = stitch(es);
st st = stocking/stockinette st;
tog = together;
WS = wrong side;
yo = yarn over needle to make a st

Instructions

LEFT BACK:

Cast on 15 sts.
1st row: (RS) K1, kfb, k to end. 16 sts.
2nd row: P to end.
3rd row: (inc row) K1, kfb, k to last 3 sts, kfb, k2. 18 sts.
Cont in st st, inc in this way at each end of next 19 RS rows. 56 sts.
** Cont in st st, (inc as before at end of next RS row and at each end of foll RS row) 3 times. 65 sts.
Cont in st st, (inc as before at end of next 2 RS rows and at each end of foll RS row) 3 times. 77 sts.
Cont in st st, inc at end of next 6 RS rows. 83 sts. Work 2 rows in st st.

Edging:

1st row: (WS) K to end.
2nd row: K2, (yo, k2tog, k1) 27 times.
3rd, 5th and 7th rows: P to end.
4th row: K1, (yo, k2tog, k1) 27 times, k1.
6th row: K3, (yo, k2tog, k1) 26 times, yo, k2tog.
8th row: As 2nd row. Cast/bind off knitwise.

RIGHT BACK:

Cast on 15 sts.
1st row: (RS) K to last 3 sts, kfb, k2. 16 sts.

2nd row: P to end.
3rd row: K1, kfb, k to last 3 sts, kfb, k2. 18 sts.
Cont in st st, inc in this way at each end of next 19 RS rows. 56 sts.
** Cont in st st, (inc as before at beg of next RS row and at each end of foll RS row) 3 times. 65 sts.
Cont in st st, (inc as before at beg of next 2 RS rows and at each end of foll RS row) 3 times. 77 sts.
Cont in st st, inc at beg of next 6 RS rows. 83 sts. Work 2 rows in st st.

Edging:

Work as given for Left back edging.

RIGHT FRONT:

Cast on 3 sts.
1st row: (RS) K1, kfb, k1. 4 sts.
2nd row: Pfb, p to end. 5 sts.
3rd row: K1, kfb, k to last 2 sts, kfb, k1. 7 sts. Work last 2 rows 3 more times, then work 2nd row again. 17 sts.
Next row: (RS) K1, kfb, k to last 2 sts, kfb, k1, cast on 7 sts. 26 sts.
P 1 row.
Next row: (RS) K1, kfb, k to last 3 sts, kfb, k2. 28 sts.
Cont in st st, inc in this way at each end

of next 14 RS rows. 56 sts.
Complete as given for Left back from ** to end.

LEFT FRONT:

Cast on 3 sts.
1st row: (RS) K1, kfb, k1. 4 sts.
2nd row: P to last 2 sts, pfb, p1. 5 sts.
3rd row: Kfb, k to last 3 sts, kfb, k2. 7 sts.
Work last 2 rows 4 more times. 19 sts.
Next row: (WS) P19, cast on 7 sts. 26 sts.
Next row: (RS) K1, kfb, k to last 3 sts, kfb, k2.
Cont in st st, inc in this way at each end of next
14 RS rows. 56 sts.
Complete as given for Right back from ** to end.

COLLAR:

Taking one st in from each side, join front, back and side
seams with mattress stitch. Darn in ends. Using circular
needle, and with RS of work facing, pick up and k 26 sts
across back neck, 20 sts down left front neck and 20 sts
up right front neck. 66 sts.
K 14 rounds. Cast/bind off knitwise.
If you prefer to work the collar on two needles, join
back, front and left side seam. With RS of work facing,
pick up and k 27 sts across back neck, 20 sts down
left front neck and 21 sts up right front neck. 68 sts.
Beg with a p row, work 15 rows in st st. Cast/bind off
knitwise. Join right side seam and collar, reversing seam
at rolled edge of collar.

FRINGE:

Cut 432 x 38cm (15in) lengths of yarn. For each tassel,
take 4 lengths of yarn, fold in half, with RS facing, and
proceed as described on the right.

HOW TO
MAKE A FRINGE

1 Take the strands of yarn and fold in half. Put a crochet hook through the eyelet hole and catch the top of the loop of folded strands with the hook.

2 Pull the looped strands up through the eyelet hole.

3 Pass the ends of the strands through the loop from back to front. Pull downwards to tighten the knot formed right up to the fabric.

4 Continue making tassels in this way until you have finished. Comb through the tassels with your fingers. Using sharp scissors, trim the tassels to an even length.

All-stripe gloves

Merino wool and three-colour stripes are a winning combination for these cosy gloves.

These fashionably striped gloves with ribbed cuffs are great for keeping your hands warm.

The Yarn
Sirdar Sublime Extra Fine Merino Wool DK contains 100% merino wool. It is a luxuriously smooth yarn with clear stitch definition that can be machine washed at a low temperature. There are plenty of subtle shades to choose from.

GETTING STARTED

Basic striped stocking/stockinette stitch fabric but pay attention to working fingers

Size:
To fit an average size woman's hand
Width above thumb: 18.5cm (7¼in)

How much yarn:
2 x 50g (2oz) balls of Sirdar Sublime Extra Fine Merino Wool DK, approx 116m (127 yards) per ball, in main colour A
1 ball (or large oddments) in each of two contrast colours B and C

Needles:
Pair of 3mm (no. 11/US 2) knitting needles
Pair of 3.75mm (no. 9/US 5) knitting needles

Tension/gauge:
23 sts and 30 rows measure 10cm (4in) square over st st on 3.75mm (no. 9/US 5) needles
IT IS ESSENTIAL TO WORK TO THE STATED TENSION/ GAUGE TO ACHIEVE SUCCESS

What you have to do:
Work cuffs in single (knit one, purl one) rib. Work main fabric in stocking/stockinette stitch and two-row stripes. Carry colours not in use loosely up side of work. Shape thumb gusset, then work thumb and fingers individually as described. Join fingers and side seam.

Abbreviations:

alt = alternate;
beg = beginning;
cm = centimetre(s);
cont = continue;
foll = following;
inc = increasing;
k = knit;
m1 = make one stitch by picking up strand lying between needles and working into back of it;
p = purl;
rem = remain(ing);
rep = repeat;
RS = right side;
st(s) = stitch(es);
st st = stocking/ stockinette stitch;
tog = together;
WS = wrong side

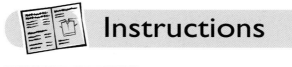

Instructions

RIGHT GLOVE:

With 3mm (no. 11/US 2) needles and A, cast on 43 sts.

1st row: (RS) K2, (p1, k1) to last st, k1.
2nd row: K1, (p1, k1) to end.
Rep last 2 rows until work measures 6cm (2½in) from beg, ending with a WS row and inc 3 sts evenly across last row. 46 sts. Change to 3.75mm (no. 9/US 5) needles. Beg with a k row, cont in st st and 8-row stripe sequence of 2 rows each A, B, A and C throughout. Work 10 rows, ending with a WS row.*

Shape thumb gusset:

1st row: K23, m1, k3, m1, k20.
2nd and foll alt rows: P to end.
3rd row: K23, m1, k5, m1, k20.
5th row: K23, m1, k7, m1, k20.
Cont in this way, inc 2 sts on every foll alt row, until there are 58 sts.
Next row: P to end.

Divide for thumb:

Next row: K38, turn.
Next row: P15, turn.
**Cont on these 15 sts, work 14 rows in st st.

Next row: (K2tog) 7 times, k1. Cut off yarn and thread through rem 8 sts, draw up and fasten off.
With RS of work facing, rejoin yarn to base of thumb and k to end. 43 sts. Work 11 rows straight, ending with a WS row.

Divide for fingers:
First finger:

Next row: K28, turn.
Next row: P13, turn and cast on 2 sts. Cont on these 15 sts, work 22 rows in st st.
Next row: (K2tog) 7 times, k1. Cut off yarn and thread through rem 8 sts, draw up and fasten off.

Second finger:

With RS of work facing, rejoin yarn to base of first finger and pick up and k 2 sts from 2 cast-on sts, k5, turn.
Next row: P12, turn and cast on 2 sts. Cont on these 14 sts and work 26 rows in st st.
Next row: (K2tog) to end. Cut off yarn and thread through rem 7 sts, draw up and fasten off.

Third finger:

With RS of work facing, rejoin yarn to

base of second finger and pick up and k 2 sts from 2 cast-on sts, k5, turn.

Next row: P12, turn and cast on 2 sts.

Complete as given for second finger, working 22 rows instead of 26.

Fourth finger:

With RS of work facing, rejoin yarn to base of third finger and pick up and k 2 sts from 2 cast-on sts, k5, turn.

Next row: P to end.

Work 16 rows in st st on these 12 sts. Complete as given for second finger.

LEFT GLOVE:

Work as given for Right glove to *.

Shape thumb gusset:

1st row: K20, m1, k3, m1, k23.

2nd and foll alt rows: P to end.

3rd row: K20, m1, k5, m1, k23.

5th row: K20, m1, k7, m1, k23.

Cont in this way, inc 2 sts on every foll alt row, until there are 58 sts.

Next row: P to end.

Divide for thumb:

Next row: K35, turn.

Next row: P15, turn.

Complte as given for Right glove from ** to end.

Making up

Using A, join all seams.

Striped scarf with pompoms

Rainbow stripes and giant pompoms at each end make this a fun scarf to wear.

Worked in stocking/stockinette stitch and multi-coloured stripes, the side edges of this scarf are sewn together to form a double thickness. The ends are then gathered up and trimmed with big pompoms.

GETTING STARTED

 *Easy stocking/stockinette stitch and stripes but fabric is double width (to be folded in half and sewn up), so working a long scarf may take a little time*

Size:
Scarf is 15cm wide x 159cm long (6in x 62½in), excluding pompoms

How much yarn:
1 x 50g (2oz) ball Wendy Mode Emu Superwash DK, approx 110m (120 yards) per ball, in each of 5 colours A, B, C, D and E
2 balls in colour F

Needles:
Pair of 4mm (no. 8/US 6) knitting needles

Tension/gauge:
22 sts and 30 rows measure 10cm (4in) square over st st on 4mm (no. 8/US 6) needles
IT IS ESSENTIAL TO WORK TO THE STATED TENSION/GAUGE TO ACHIEVE SUCCESS

What you have to do:
Work in stocking/stockinette stitch. Follow stripe pattern. Join in and cut off colours as required. Make pompoms to trim ends of scarf.

The Yarn
Emu Superwash DK from Wendy Mode is a classic 100% wool yarn with a practical twist – it can be machine washed. There are over 30 shades to choose from so you can have a lot of fun with choosing the colour combinations for your stripes.

Abbreviations:
beg = beginning;
cont = continue;
cm = centimetre(s);
foll = follows;
k = knit;
patt = pattern;
rep = repeat;
RS = right side;
st(s) = stitch(es);
st st = stocking/
stockinette stitch;
WS = wrong side.

Instructions

SCARF:

With 4mm (no. 8/US 6) needles and A, cast on 67 sts. Beg with a k row, cont in st st and stripe patt, joining in and cutting off colours as required as foll:

1st–6th rows: In A.
7th–10th rows: In B.
11th–12th rows: In C.
13th–20th rows: In D.
21st and 22nd rows: In E.
23rd–28th rows: In F.
29th–32nd rows: In A.
33rd and 34th rows: In B.
35th–42nd rows: In C.
43rd and 44th rows: In D.
45th–50th rows: In E.
51st–54th rows: In F.
55th and 56th rows: In A.
57th–64th rows: In B.
65th and 66th rows: In C.
67th–72nd rows: In D.
73rd–76th rows: In E.
77th and 78th rows: In F.
79th–86th rows: In A.
87th and 88th rows: In B.
89th–94th rows: In C.
95th–98th rows: In D.

99th and 100th rows: In E.
101st–108th rows: In F.
109th and 110th rows: In A.
111th–116th rows: In B.
117th–120th rows: In C.
121st and 122nd rows: In D.
123rd–130th rows: In E.
131st and 132nd rows: In F.

These 132 rows form stripe patt. Rep them twice more, then work 1st–50th rows again, ending on WS of stripe in E. Cast/bind off.

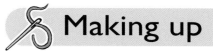 # Making up

Press carefully according to directions on ball band. With RS facing, fold scarf in half and join long seam with backstitch. Turn scarf through to RS, placing seam down centre of one side. Work a row of gathering stitches around cast-on and cast/bound-off edges of scarf, pull up tightly and fasten off securely.

With F, make 2 pompoms, each 10cm (4in) in diameter. Sew a pompom securely to each end of the scarf.

HOW TO
MAKE A POMPOM

Use this technique to make the large pompoms at each end of the scarf.

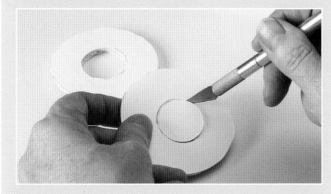

1 These pompoms are 10cm (4in) in diameter. Cut two circles of thick cardboard that are slightly larger than the diameter of the finished pompom. Cut a circle from the centre of each disc.

2 Thread a large-eyed sewing needle with as many ends of yarn as you can fit through the eye. Each length of yarn should be approximately 1m (1 yard) long.

3 Hold the two discs one on top of the other. Thread the needle through the centre and hold the ends of the yarn with one thumb. Take the needle around the discs and back through the centre. Continue to do this working your way evenly around the discs until the centre hole is full.

4 Using small sharp scissors, cut around the outside edge of the discs, snipping through all the layers of yarn.

5 Gently ease the discs apart so that there is a straight section of yarn visible between them. Take a small piece of yarn and tie it firmly around the middle of the pompom, knotting it as tightly as possible.

6 Ease the discs off the pompom and fluff it up into a round shape. Trim around the pompom, turning it as you work, to give an even shape.

Felted bobble cushion

Raised bobbles and a felted fabric provide an interesting mix of contrasting textures.

This cushion/pillow cover is worked in stocking/stockinette stitch and enlivened with lines of alternating contrast-coloured bobbles. The finished effect is achieved by felting in a washing machine.

The Yarn
Simply Wool is 100% pure wool. Its softly spun fibres are ideal for felting and there are plenty of shades to choose for coordinating colour work.

GETTING STARTED

Practise making bobbles first, then knitting this cushion/pillow should be straightforward, although felting a fabric is often unpredictable

Size:
Cushion/pillow is approximately 40cm x 40cm (16in x 16in)

How much yarn:
4 x 100g (3½oz) balls of Simply Wool DK, approx 200m (219 yards) per ball, in main colour A
1 ball in each of three contrast colours B, C and D

Needles:
Pair of 3.75mm (no. 9/US 5) knitting needles

Additional items:
1 x 2cm (¾in) wide button
40cm x 40cm (16in x 16in) cushion pad/pillow form

Tension/gauge:
21 sts and 29 rows measure 10cm (4in) square over st st BEFORE felting on 3.75mm (no. 9/US 5) needles

What you have to do:
For front, work in stocking/stockinette stitch with main colour, making coloured bobbles as directed at intervals. Weave in bobble yarn not in use across wrong side of work. Make back sections in stocking/stockinette stitch with garter-stitch border at one edge. On one back section, work vertical buttonhole inside garter-stitch border. Felt finished cover in a washing machine.

Abbreviations:
beg = beginning;
cm = centimetre(s);
cont = continue;
foll = follows;
g st = garter stitch (every row knit);
k = knit;
p = purl;
rem = remaining;
rep = repeat;
RS = right side;
sl = slip;
st(s) = stitch(es);
st st = stocking/stockinette stitch;
tog = together;
WS = wrong side

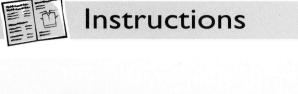

Instructions

FRONT:
With A, cast on 104 sts. Beg with a p row, work 23 rows in st st, ending with a WS row.
Red bobble row: (RS) K22 A, * make bobble (mb) as foll: using two ends of B, k into (front and back) twice of next st (making 4 sts out of 1), turn; p into front and back of next st, p2, p into front and back of next st, turn; beg with a k row, work 5 rows in st st on these 6 sts, turn; p2tog, p2, p2tog, turn; sl 2nd, 3rd and 4th sts over first st and off left-hand needle, then k rem st with A, k19 A, rep from * twice more weaving in bobble yarn not in use across WS of work, using B, mb, k21 A. Cut off B.
Cont in A only and beg with a p row, work 21 rows in st st, ending with a WS row.
Pink bobble row: (RS) K32 A, *using two ends of C, mb, k19 A, rep from * once more, using C, mb, k31 A. Cut off C.
Cont in A only and beg with a p row, work

21 rows in st st, ending with a WS row.
Orange bobble row: (RS) Using two ends of D for bobbles, work as given for red bobble row. Cut off D.
Cont in A only and beg with a p row, work 21 rows in st st, ending with a WS row.
Pink bobble row: (RS) Work as given for pink bobble row. Cut off C.
Cont in A only and beg with a p row, work 21 rows in st st, ending with a WS row.
Red bobble row: (RS) Work as given for red bobble row. Cut off B.
Cont in A only and beg with a p row, work 21 rows in st st, ending with a WS row.
Cast/bind off.

BACK: (With buttonhole)
With A, cast on 65 sts.
1st row: (WS) Sl 1, k5, p to end.
2nd row: K to end.
Rep these 2 rows 30 times more.
Make buttonhole as foll:

Next 2 rows: Sl 1, k5, turn and k6.

Rep these 2 rows twice more.

Next row: Sl 1, k5, cut off yarn and leave sts on needle. With WS of work facing, rejoin yarn to main fabric and p to end. Work 6 rows st st on main fabric.

Next row: (RS) K to end across main fabric, then across 6 sts of band.

Cont in st st with g st border as before, work 63 more rows, ending with a WS row. Cast/bind off.

BACK: (Without buttonhole)

With A, cast on 65 sts.

1st row: (WS) Sl 1, k5, p to end.

2nd row: K to end.

Rep these 2 rows 65 times more, then work 1st row again, ending with a WS row. Cast/bind off.

 # Making up

Pin and block to shape. Place cushion/pillow front WS down on a flat surface. Lay cushion/pillow back with buttonhole RS down on top of cushion/pillow front and then other cushion/pillow back RS down on rem section of front, overlapping backs in the centre. Using a backstitch seam, join all around outer edges.

Felting:

With cushion/pillow cover WS out, place in a washing machine with other items for extra agitation. Wash at 30°C (86°F), remove from machine and check size. If cover still needs to be smaller, then wash again. Shape cover while still damp and allow to dry thoroughly.

Turn cover RS out. Sew on button and insert cushion pad/pillow form. Button to close.

Soft cape

Elegant and understated, this beautiful mohair cape creates a classic evening look.

This neat little cape in stocking/stockinette stitch and a beautiful mohair yarn has a soft collar that loosely drapes around the neckline.

GETTING STARTED

Working on circular needles and the large number of stitches may take some getting used to

Size:

One size fits bust: 81–97cm (32–38in)

Length from lower edge to collar: 33cm (13in)

How much yarn:

8 x 25g (1oz) balls of Rowan Kidsilk Aura in Pumice, approx 75m (82 yards) per ball

Needles:

4mm (no. 8/US 6) circular knitting needle

4.5mm (no. 7/US 7) circular knitting needle

Additional items:

Stitch markers

Tension/gauge:

19 sts and 27 rows measure 10cm (4in) square over st st on 4.5mm (no. 7/US 7) needles

IT IS ESSENTIAL TO WORK TO THE STATED TENSION/ GAUGE TO ACHIEVE SUCCESS

What you have to do:

Use circular needles to hold large number of stitches and work in rounds. Work main fabric in stocking/ stockinette stitch (every round knit). Work collar in garter stitch (knit one round and purl one round). Use paired shaping at intervals to shape cape. Increase at start of collar to give loose shape to fold down.

The Yarn

Rowan Kidsilk Aura is a blend of 75% mohair and 25% silk. It can be hand-washed at a cool temperature and there is a range of contemporary subtle colours to choose from.

Abbreviations:
beg = beginning;
cm = centimetre(s);
cont = continue;
dec = decrease;
k = knit;
m1 = make one stitch
by picking up strand lying
between needles and
working into back of it;
p = purl;
psso = pass slipped
stitch over;
st(s) = stitch(es);
sl = slip;
st st = stocking/
stockinette stitch;
tog = together

 # Instructions

CAPE:

With 4mm (no. 8/US 6) circular needle cast on 300 sts loosely. Marking beg of each round, work 4 rounds in k1, p1 rib. Change to 4.5mm (no. 7/US 7) circular needle and work 36 rounds in st st (every round k).

1st dec round: (K2tog, k26, sl 1, k1, psso) 10 times. 280 sts. Work 11 rounds straight.

2nd dec round: (K2tog, k24, sl 1, k1, psso) 10 times. 260 sts. Work 9 rounds straight.

3rd dec round: (K2tog, k22, sl 1, k1, psso) 10 times. 240 sts. Work 7 rounds straight.

4th dec round: (K2tog, k20, sl 1, k1, psso) 10 times. 220 sts. Work 3 rounds straight.

5th dec round: (K2tog, k18, sl 1, k1, psso) 10 times. 200 sts.

Work 3 rounds straight.

6th dec round: (K2tog, k16, sl 1, k1, psso) 10 times. 180 sts. Work 3 rounds straight.

7th dec round: (K2tog, k14, sl 1, k1, psso) 10 times. 160 sts. Work 3 rounds straight.

8th dec round: (K2tog, k12, sl 1, k1, psso) 10 times. 140 sts. Work 3 rounds straight.

Collar:

Next round: (K1, m1, k12, m1, k1) 10 times. 160 sts.

Cont in garter st (1 round k, 1 round p) for 15cm (6in).

Cast/bind off loosely.

HOW TO
USE CIRCULAR NEEDLES

A circular needle is used to make a tubular piece of knitting, as you knit round in a continuous circle. You can cast on and knit whole items on circular needles or use them to pick up stitches and knit a neck or a round shape. Circular needles consist of two short straight needles joined by a flexible plastic wire. They are available in sizes just like ordinary knitting needles and they also come in several lengths; the needles and connecting wire should be short enough so the stitches are not stretched when joined.

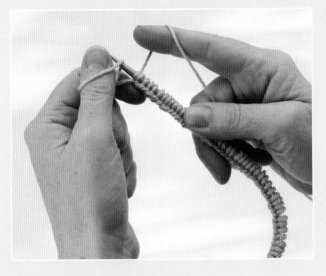

1 Cast on or pick up stitches as you would for ordinary knitting using a regular needle. Distribute the stitches evenly around the needles and wire, making sure they all lie in the same direction and are not twisted

3 Hold the needle with the last cast-on stitch in your right hand and the needle with the first cast-on stitch in your left hand. Knit the first cast-on stitch, keeping the yarn well tensioned to avoid a gap.

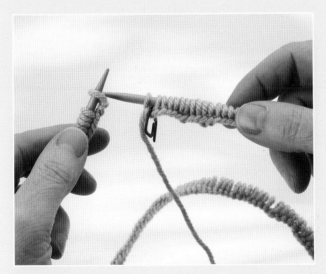

2 The last cast-on stitch is the last stitch of the round. Place a marker here to indicate the end of the round.

4 Work until you reach the marker, checking that the stitches are eased around the needles as you work. This completes the first round. Continue knitting in this way for the required depth of the fabric tube.

Skinny scarf

This scarf takes no time at all and it will soon become one of your favourite knits.

Make this trendy openwork scarf on big needles with cotton yarn and very little effort – the drop-stitch pattern will quickly develop as you knit.

The Yarn

Sirdar Luxury Soft Cotton is 100% cotton yarn in a double knitting (light worsted) weight. It is a delight to work with and feels soft next to the skin. There is a beautiful colour range with chalky pastels and muted darker shades that make choosing three complementary shades for the scarf an easy task.

GETTING STARTED

Simple to knit in a straight strip and stripes. Drop-stitch pattern can often look untidy until the openwork pattern begins to develop

Size:

Scarf is 13cm wide and 220cm long (5in x 86in)

How much yarn:

1 x 50g (2oz) ball of Sirdar Luxury Soft Cotton DK, approx 95m (104 yards) per ball, in each of three colours A, B and C

Needles:

Pair of 5mm (no. 6/US 8) knitting needles

Tension/gauge:

13 sts and 13 rows measure 10cm (4in) square in patt on 5mm (no. 6/US 8) needles

IT IS ESSENTIAL TO WORK TO THE STATED TENSION/ GAUGE TO ACHIEVE SUCCESS

What you have to do:

Cast on very loosely. Work drop-stitch pattern by winding yarn twice around needle on one row and dropping extra loops on the following row. Work striped pattern. Carry contrast yarns up side of work. Cast/bind off loosely.

Instructions

Abbreviations:
cm = centimetre(s);
cont = continue;
k = knit;
patt = pattern;
rep = repeat;
st(s) = stitch(es)

SCARF:

With A, cast on 17 sts loosely.

1st row: K to end.

2nd row: K to end, winding yarn twice around needle for every st.

3rd row: K to end, dropping extra loops.

These 3 rows form drop-stitch patt.

Join in B. Cont in patt, work 3 rows in B, always catching contrast yarn (by twisting together with working yarn) from 2 rows down at side edges before every row.

Join in C. Cont in patt, work 3 rows in C, catching yarn at sides as before.

These 9 rows form striped patt. Rep them until work measures about 220cm (86in), ending after a 3rd patt row. Cast/bind off loosely.

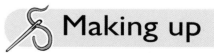

Making up

Weave in any loose ends along stitches in the same colour as yarn. Do not press.

HOW TO
WORK THE DROP STITCH PATTERN

To begin with, working a pattern where you have to drop stitches off the needle can feel odd, but once you see the openwork pattern developing it makes sense of the technique. This is a quick and easy stitch to work and your scarf will grow at a surprising rate.

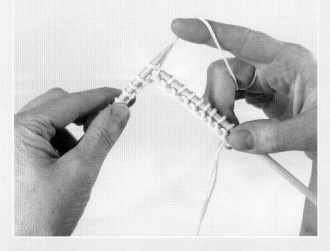

1 Cast on the required number of stitches loosely. The cast-on edge should not pull the edge of the scarf in as the pattern develops. Although the cast-on stitches must be loose, they should also be even. Knit the first row.

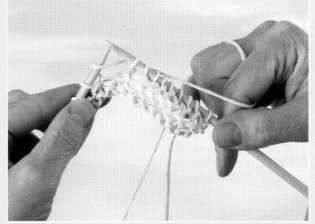

3 Knit to the end of the next row, dropping the extra loop off the left-hand needle on each stitch. This forms the openwork part of the pattern.

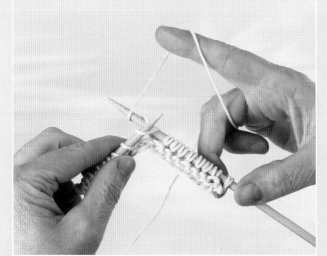

2 Knit the next row but wrap the yarn twice around the right-hand needle (as shown) each time you make a knit stitch. This will give you a row of double loops for each stitch.

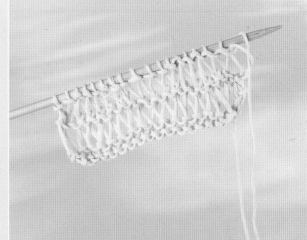

4 These three rows form the pattern and are repeated for the length of the scarf. This creates a row of open stitches intersected by a row of garter stitch. Change colours as instructed in the pattern to create the stripes in this scarf.

Fair Isle bobble hat

Muted shades of blue, lilac and cream make a great combination worked in traditional Fair Isle pattern.

Keep cosy with this traditional hat trimmed with a pompom and featuring a ribbed brim and bands of subtle Fair Isle patterns.

GETTING STARTED

This is a good design to try out your Fair Isle knitting skills

Size:
To fit an average size adult head

How much yarn:
2 x 50g (2oz) balls of Debbie Bliss Rialto Aran, approx 80m (87 yards) per ball, in main colour A
1 ball in each of two contrast colours B and C

Needles:
Pair of 4.5mm (no. 7/US 7) knitting needles
Pair of 5mm (no. 6/US 8) knitting needles

Tension/gauge:
18 sts and 24 rows measure 10cm (4in) square over st st on 5mm (no. 6/US 8) needles
IT IS ESSENTIAL TO WORK TO THE STATED TENSION/ GAUGE TO ACHIEVE SUCCESS

What you have to do:
Work brim in double (knit two, purl two) rib. Work main fabric in stocking/stockinette stitch with bands of Fair Isle pattern, stranding yarn not in use across wrong side of work. Shape crown by working decrease rows at regular intervals. Make pompom and stitch to top of hat.

The Yarn
Debbie Bliss Rialto Aran is 100% merino wool. It produces a smooth stocking/ stockinette stitch fabric with good stitch definition and it can be machine washed at a low temperature. There are plenty of fabulous shades to choose from.

Abbreviations:

beg = beginning;
cm = centimetre(s);
cont = continue;
dec = decreasing;
foll = follows;
k = knit;
p = purl;
patt = pattern;
psso = pass slipped stitch over;
rem = remaining;
rep = repeat;
RS = right side;
sl = slip;
st(s) = stitch(es);
st st = stocking/stockinette stitch;
tog = together;
WS = wrong side

Instructions

HAT:

With 4.5mm (no. 7/US 7) needles and A, cast on 122 sts.

1st row: K2, (p2, k2) to end.
2nd row: P2, (k2, p2) to end.
Rep these 2 rows 15 times more, dec 1 st at centre of last row. 121 sts.
Change to 5mm (no. 6/US 8) needles. Beg with a k row, work 2 rows in st st. Cont in st st and Fair Isle patt 1 as foll, stranding yarn not in use loosely across WS of work:
1st row: (RS) K2 A, (1 B, 3 A) to last 3 sts, 1 B, 2 A.
2nd row: P1 A, (3 B, 1 A) to end.
3rd row: K2 B, (1 C, 3 B) to last 3 sts, 1 C, 2 B.
4th row: P1 A, (1 C, 1 A) to end.
5th row: As 3rd row.

6th row: As 2nd row.
7th row: As 1st row.
8th row: With A, p to end.
1st dec row: With A, k3, (sl 1, k2tog, psso, k5) to last 6 sts, sl 1, k2tog, psso, k3. 91 sts.
Next row: With A, p to end.
Cont in Fair Isle patt 2 as foll:
1st row: (RS) K1 A, (1 C, 1 A) to end.
2nd row: P1 C, (1 B, 1 C) to end.
3rd row: As 1st row.
4th row: With A, p to end.
2nd dec row: With A, k1, (k2tog, k1) to end. 61 sts.
Next row: With A, p to end.
Work 8 rows in Fair Isle patt 1, reading B for C and C for B.
3rd dec row: With A, k1, (k2tog) to end. 31 sts.

Next row: With A, p to end.
Work 4 rows in Fair Isle patt 2, reading B for C and C for B.
4th dec row: With A, k1, (k2tog) to end. 16 sts.
Next row: With A, (p2tog) to end. 8 sts.
Cut off yarn, thread through rem sts, draw up and fasten off securely.

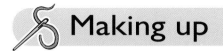

Making up

Join back seam, reversing seam on last 22 rows of rib to fold back brim. Make a pompom approximately 7cm (2¾in) in diameter from A, B and C and attach securely to top of hat.

Dotty tea cosy

Bring a touch of 1930s nostalgia to your tea table with this pastel tea cosy decorated with bright buttons.

Tea is always trendy and now your tea cosy can be as well! Knit this simple shape in chunky yarn in sizes that can be adjusted for small, medium and large teapots. Add dotty decoration with pairs of bright-coloured buttons.

GETTING STARTED

 Easy stitches worked in chunky yarn on big needles make this a great project for a beginner

Size:

Tea pot circumference: 33[40:49]cm/13[15¾:19¼]in, excluding spout

Height: 17[18:21]cm/6¾[7:8¼]in (adjustable)

Note: Figures in square brackets [ ] refer to larger sizes; where there is only one set of figures, it applies to all sizes

How much yarn:

1 x 100g (3½oz) ball of Rowan Cocoon, approx 115m (126 yards) per ball

Needles:

Pair of 6.5mm (no. 3/US 10½) knitting needles

Additional items:

Selection of flat, bright-coloured buttons – approximately 14cm x 2.5cm (1in x ⅝in) wide

Selection of bright-coloured sewing threads and needle

10cm (4in) length of 7mm (¼in) wide ribbon

Large-eyed needle

Tension/gauge:

12.5 sts and 18 rows measure 10cm (4in) square over st st on 6.5mm (no. 3/US 10½) needles

IT IS ESSENTIAL TO WORK TO THE STATED TENSION/ GAUGE TO ACHIEVE SUCCESS

What you have to do:

Work two rows in single (k1, p1) rib. Work main fabric in stocking/stockinette stitch. Knit two stitches together to shape top. Sew on buttons to decorate.

The Yarn

Rowan Cocoon is a chunky-weight yarn in a blend of 80% wool and 20% kid mohair. Wonderfully soft, it creates a fantastic texture finish. There is a small colour palette of soft or strong chalky shades to choose from.

Abbreviations:

beg = beginning;
cm = centimetre(s);
k = knit;
p = purl;
rem = remaining;
rep = repeat;
RS = right side;
st(s) = stitch(es);
st st = stocking/
stockinette stitch;
tog = together

Instructions

BACK:

Cast on 21[25:31] sts.
1st row: (RS) K1, *p1, k1, rep from * to end.
2nd row: P1, *k1, p1, rep from * to end.
Beg with a k row, work 13[14:16] cm/5[5½:6¼]in in st st, ending with a p row. (Measure work against your teapot – cosy should be approximately 4cm (1½in) below top of teapot lid. Add or take back rows to fit.)

Shape top:

3rd size only:
Next row: (K3, k2tog) 6 times, k1. 25 sts.
P 1 row.

All sizes:
Next row: (K2, k2tog) 5[6:6] times, k1. 16[19:19] sts.
P 1 row.
Next row: (K1, k2tog) 5[6:6] times, k1. 11[13:13] sts.
P 1 row.

Next row: (K2tog) 5[6:6] times, k1. 6[7:7] sts.
P 1 row.
Next row: (K2tog) 3 times, k0[1:1]. 3[4:4] sts.
Cut off yarn and thread through rem sts. Pull up tightly and fasten off.

FRONT:

Work as given for Back.

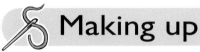 ## Making up

Press according to directions on ball band.
Sew buttons in pairs, small button on top of
a larger one, randomly over both sides of
cosy, using a separate length of thread for
each pair of buttons.

Join side seams for 5cm (2in) from cast-on
edge. Join side seams from top to start of
shaping, leaving two gaps for the handle and
spout. Try cosy on the teapot, making sure
gaps are big enough, and adjust if necessary.
Thread looped ribbon into large-eyed
needle and push through tea cosy top from
the inside. Adust loop on the outside, then
secure ribbon ends inside cosy.

Tea-time treats

Have some fun knitting these cakes, which would make a great present for a sweet-toothed friend.

For cakes that look good and won't spoil your waistline, try a plateful of these decorative goodies worked in 4-ply/fingering yarn.

GETTING STARTED

These cakes require a lot of attention to detail for a good finish and appearance

Size:
Battenburg/checkerboard cake: 6cm x 5.5cm (2½in x 2¼in); Chocolate cake: 7cm wide x 10cm long (2¾in x 4in); Cupcake: 7cm in diameter x 8cm high (2¾in x 3¼in); Frosted cakes: 4cm x 4.5cm x 2.5cm (1½in x 1¾in x 1in); Doughnut: 7.5cm (3in) in diameter

How much yarn:
1 x 50g (2oz) ball of Patons Gold Diploma 4-ply, approx 184m (201 yards) per ball, in each of nine colours A, B, C, D, E, F, G, H and I
1 x 100g (3½oz) ball of Patons Baby Fab! 4-ply, approx 375m (410 yards) per ball, in each of two colours J and K

Needles:
Pair of 3mm (no. 11/US 2½) knitting needles
Set of four short 3mm (no. 11/US 2½) double-pointed needles (Cupcake and Doughnut)

Additional items:
Polyester toy filling
Cardboard disc, 3.5cm (1½in) in diameter (Cupcake)
Oddment of dark pink yarn (Battenburg/checkerboard)
Selection of 2mm bugle beads in pink, yellow and blue (Doughnut)
Sewing needle and thread (for beads only)

Tension/gauge:
28 sts and 36 rows measure 10cm (4in) square over st st on 3mm (no. 11/US 2½) needles
IT IS ESSENTIAL TO WORK TO THE STATED TENSION/GAUGE TO ACHIEVE SUCCESS

What you have to do:
Work in colours specified and simple stitches, including garter stitch, stocking/stockinette stitch and reverse stocking/stockinette stitch. Follow instructions for simple increasing or decreasing to shape cakes. Make bobbles for 'cherries'. Decorate finished cakes with simple embroidery or add beads.

The Yarn
Patons Diploma Gold 4-ply is a practical mixture of 55% wool, 25% acrylic and 20% nylon. The wool-rich content of the yarn produces a good-looking fabric and there are plenty of fabulous colours to choose from.

Instructions

Abbreviations:

beg = beginning; **cm** = centimetre(s); **cont** = continue; **dec** = decrease(ing); **foll** = following; **g st** = garter stitch (every row knit); **inc** = increase(ing); **k** = knit; **m1** = make 1 stitch by picking up strand lying between needles and working into back of it; **p** = purl; **psso** = pass slipped stitch over; **rem** = remain(ing); **rep** = repeat; **RS** = right side; **sl** = slip; **st(s)** = stitch(es); **st st** = stocking/stockinette stitch; **tog** = together; **WS** = wrong side; **yfwd** = yarn forward/yarn over to make a stitch

BATTENBURG/CHECKERBOARD CAKE:
Square ends of cake:

With 3mm (no. 11/US 2½) needles, cast on 8 sts in A and 8 sts in B. 16 sts. Beg with a p row, work 10 rows in reverse st st, twisting yarns tog on WS of work when changing colour to avoid holes forming. Cut off yarn.

Next row: (RS) K8 B, 8 A. Beg with a k row, work 9 more rows in reverse st st with colours as set. Cast/bind off with colours as set. Work a second piece to match, but swapping colours on cast-on row and halfway through piece as before.

Edging:

With 3mm (no. 11/US 2½) needles and C, cast on 5 sts. Work 80 rows in st st. Cast/bind off.

CHOCOLATE CAKE:
Top, end and bottom:

With 3mm (no. 11/US 2½) needles and E, cast on 2 sts.
1st row: K and inc in both sts. 4 sts. Beg with a p row, cont in st st, inc 1 st at each end of every foll 4th row until there are 20 sts. Work 2 more rows in st st, ending with a k row.
Next row: K to end to mark foldline.
Beg with a k row, work 19 more rows st st.
Next row: K to end to mark foldline.
Beg with a k row, work 2 more rows in st st. Cut off E and join in D. Work 2 rows in st st.
Next row: (RS) Sl 1, k1, psso, k to last 2 sts, k2tog. Cont to dec in this way on every foll 4th row until 2 sts rem.
Next row: Sl 1, k1, psso and fasten off.

Sides:

With 3mm (no. 11/US 2½) needles, cast on 2 sts in E, 48 sts in D, 2 sts in E. 52 sts.
1st row: (RS) K2 E, p48 D, k2 E.

2nd row: P2 E, k48 D, p2 E. Rep these 2 rows twice more.
Next row: K2 E, 48 D, 2 E.
Next row: P2 E, 48 F, 2 E.
Next row: K to end in E.
Next row: P2 E, 48 D, 2 E. Work 1st and 2nd rows twice more, then work 1st row again. Cut off D.

Topping:

Cont in E only, p 1 row and k 1 row. Cast/bind off.

Big cream swirls: (Make 2)

With 3mm (no. 11/US 2) needles and C, cast on 20 sts.
1st row: K, inc in each st. 40 sts.
P 1 row and k 1 row. Cast/bind off.

Small cream swirl:

As big cream swirl, but cast on 8 sts and inc to 16 sts.

Cherries: (Make 3)

With 3mm (no. 11/US 2½) needles and F, make a slip loop on needle.
1st row: (K1, p1) twice and k1 all into slip loop. 5 sts.
2nd row: K, inc in each st. 10 sts.
P 1 row, k 1 row and p 1 row.
Next row: (K2tog) 5 times, then pass 2nd, 3rd, 4th and 5th sts over first st and off needle and fasten off.

FROSTED CAKES:
Base and 1st side:

With 3mm (no. 11/US 2½) and K, cast on 10 sts. Beg with a k row, work 13 rows in st st. Cut off K and join in A or J. Work 9 more rows in st st, ending with a p row. Cut off yarn.

Next row: With A or J, cast on 7 sts, k across 10 sts already on needle, turn and cast on 7 sts. 24 sts.

Top, 2nd and 3rd sides:
1st row: P to end.
2nd row: K to end.
3rd row: P11, (m1, p1) twice, m1, p11.
4th row: K to end.
5th row: P16, turn and k5, turn and p to end.
6th row: K to end.
7th and 8th rows: As 5th and 6th rows.
9th row: P11, (p2tog) 3 times, p10.
10th row: K to end.
11th row: P to end.
12th row: Cast/bind off 7 sts, k10, Cast/bind off 7 sts.
4th side:
Beg with a p row, work 9 rows in st st. Cast/bind off.
Case:
With 3mm (no. 11/US 2½) needles and K, cast on 9 sts.
Work 70 rows in g st. Cast/bind off.

CUPCAKE:
With 3mm (no. 11/US 2) double-pointed needles and G,
cast on 15 sts evenly over 3 needles.
1st round: (K1, m1) to end. 30 sts.
2nd and 3rd rounds: K to end.
4th round: *(K2, m1) 6 times, k3, m1, rep from * once
more. 44 sts.
5th and 6th rounds: K to end. Cont in rounds of k1, p1
rib, work in stripes as foll: 3 rounds G, 1 round H, 7 rounds
G, 1 round H and 3 rounds G. Cont in G, k 3 rounds.
Next round: (picot) (Yfwd, k2tog) to end.
K 3 rounds, then k 4 rounds in E.
Next round: (K9, k2tog) to end. 40 sts.
Cut off E and cont in G.
Next round: (K8, k2tog) to end.
Next round: (K7, k2tog) to end.
Cont to dec in this way on every round until 8 sts rem.
Next round: (K2tog) 4 times. Cut off yarn. Thread cut
end through rem 4 sts, draw up and fasten off securely.
Cherry:
Make 1 cherry as given for Chocolate Cake.

DOUGHNUT:
With 3mm (no. 11/US 2½) double-pointed needles and E, cast
on 30 sts evenly over 3 needles. K 6 rounds (to form st st).
Next round: (K2, inc in next st) to end. 40 sts.
K 8 more rounds. Cut off E and join in I. K 11 rounds.
Next round: (K2, k2tog) to end. 30 sts. K 2 more rounds.
Cut off I and join in E. K 4 rounds. Cast/bind off.

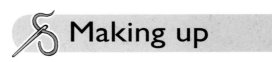

Making up

BATTENBURG/CHECKERBOARD CAKE:
Press according to directions. Join ends of edging strip tog.
With RS facing, pin, then stitch edging around one square
end. Repeat for other square end, leaving a gap in seam for
turning through. Turn through and insert stuffing, then slip
stitch seam closed. Work backstitch over colour change
lines on square ends with darker pink yarn.

CHOCOLATE CAKE:
Press according to directions. Find and mark centre of side
sections on cast-on and cast/bound-off edges. With point
of cast-on edge of top to marker on cast/bound-off edge of
side section, so matching parts in E, join seam, placing final
marker at point of bottom section and leaving a small gap.
Insert stuffing and close gap. Sew on cherries after stuffing
slightly. Twist cream swirls and sew on.

FROSTED CAKES:
Press st st sections according to directions. Join row ends
of sides to cast-on or cast/bound-off edges of top, then
sew two of the three edges around base (white square) to
upper section. Stuff firmly and slip stitch open edge closed.
Join cast-on and cast/bound-off edges of case and stitch
around sides of base. Backstitch lines in a contrast colour
across top as shown in picture.

CUPCAKE:
Fold case at picot edge and sew through last row in K
before change to E, working through both thicknesses to
form edge of case. Insert filling through opening at base of
case, then add cardboard disc to form flat bottom. Run a
gathering thread through cast-on row, draw up and fasten
off. Sew on cherry.

DOUGHNUT:
With RS of work facing, join cast/bound-off round to cast-
on round, leaving a small gap for filling. Insert filling and slip
stitch opening closed. Sew on beads at random over 'iced/
frosted' section, sewing on two at a time and more densely
over top of doughnut.

Cuddly hot-water bottle cover

Knitted in ultra-soft yarn, this hot-water bottle cover will be yet another excuse for staying in bed!

Button up your hot-water bottle in this soft cover that has a pretty broken stripe effect and enjoy the cosy warmth.

The Yarn

Rowan Cocoon is a luxurious mix of 80% merino wool and 20% kid mohair and creates a beautiful textured finish. The colours are soft and smoky.

GETTING STARTED

 Chunky yarn knits up quickly and colour work is simple with easy slip-stitch pattern

Size:
To fit a standard hot-water bottle
38cm (15in) 45cm (17¾in)

How much yarn:
2 x 100g (3½oz) balls of Rowan Cocoon, approx 115m (126 yards) per ball, in colour A
1 ball in colour B

Needles:
Pair of 5.5mm (no. 5/US 9) knitting needles
Pair of 6.5mm (no. 3/US 10½) knitting needles

Additional items:
1 large button

Tension/gauge:
12 sts and 19 rows measure 10cm (4in) square over patt on 6.5mm (no. 3/US 10½) needles
IT IS ESSENTIAL TO WORK TO THE STATED TENSION/GAUGE TO ACHIEVE SUCCESS

What you have to do:
Work in stocking/stockinette stitch incorporating second colour with slip-stitch pattern. Use simple shaping for side edges. Work top and back opening borders in garter stitch. Make a buttonhole by casting/binding off and casting on stitches.

Instructions

Abbreviations:

= beginning; = centimetre(s); = continue; = follows; = garter stitch (every row knit); = knit; = make one stitch by picking up bar lying between needles and working into back of it; = purl; = pattern; = purlwise; = repeat; = right side; = stitch(es); = slip; = stocking/stockinette stitch; = together; = wrong side; = yarn to back; = yarn to front

FRONT:

With 6.5mm (no. 3/US 10½) needles and A, cast on 21 sts.
P1 row.
(RS) K1, m1, k to last st, m1, k1.
Cast on 2 sts, p to last st, m1, p1.
Cast on 2 sts, k to last st, m1, k1. 29 sts.
Beg with a p row, work 5 rows in st st, ending with a p row. Cont in patt as foll:
With B, k2, (sl 1 pwise, k2) to end.
With B, k2, (ytf, sl 1 pwise, ytb, k2) to end.
As 1st and 2nd rows.
With A and beg with a k row,
work in st st.
These 12 rows form patt.* Rep them twice more, then work 1st–4th rows again.
** Cont in A only and beg with a k row, work 6 rows in st st.

Shape top:

(RS) Cast/bind off 2 sts, k to last 2 sts, k2tog.
Cast/bind off 2 sts, p to last 2 sts, p2tog.
Rep last 2 rows once more. 17 sts. Work 20 rows in g st. Cast/bind off.

BACK:
Lower part:

Work as given for Front to *.
Rep last 12 rows once more, then work 1st–4th rows again.
Cont in A only and beg with a k row, work3 rows in st st.
Change to 5.5mm (no. 5/US 9) needles. Work 5 rows in g st. Cast/bind off.

Upper part:

With 5.5mm (no. 5/US 9) needles and A, cast on 29 sts.
K2 rows.
K13, cast/bind off next 3 sts,
k to end.
K to end, casting on 3 sts over those cast/bound off in previous row.
K2 more rows.
Change to 6.5mm (no. 3/US 10½) needles. Beg with a k row, work 2 rows in st st, then work 1st–4th patt rows.
Now complete as given for Front from ** to end.

Making up

Lay front WS down. Place upper back on front RS down, matching cast/bound-off edges. Place lower back on front RS down, matching cast-on edges and overlapping g st bands in centre. Join front to back by sewing all around outer edge. Turn RS out. Sew on button.

Fair Isle socks

These cosy comfortable socks are equally at home trekking in the hills or chilling on the sofa.

Comfortable for walking shoes or boots, these Aran- (fisherman) weight socks are worked in stocking/stockinette stitch and have Fair Isle-patterned turn-back cuffs.

GETTING STARTED

Most socks are worked in the round on sets of needles. These are easier to work on two needles but still need a lot of shaping

Size:

Length from heel to toe: 21.5cm (8½in)

Height from heel to top of cuff (turned back): 21cm (8¼in)

How much yarn:

2 x 100g (3½oz) balls of Wendy Mode Aran, approx 200m (219 yards) per ball, in main colour M

1 ball in contrast colour C

Needles:

Pair of 3.75mm (no. 9/US 5) knitting needles

Pair of 4mm (no. 8/US 6) knitting needles

Additional items:

3 stitch holders

Tension/gauge:

21 sts and 27 rows measure 10cm (4in) square over st st on 4mm (no. 8/US 6) needles

IT IS ESSENTIAL TO WORK TO THE STATED TENSION/ GAUGE TO ACHIEVE SUCCESS

What you have to do:

Work in stocking/stockinette stitch. Work two-colour Fair Isle pattern from chart, carrying yarn not in use across back of work. Work simple decreasing and turning rows for shaping. Cast/bind off two sets of stitches together.

The Yarn

Wendy Mode Aran is a practical mixture of natural and man-made fibres with 50% wool and 50% acrylic that can be machine washed. It is available in a small range of colours that are perfect for making socks.

Abbreviations:

beg = beginning;
cm = centimetre(s);
cont = continue;
foll = follows;
k = knit;
p = purl;
patt = pattern;
psso = pass slipped stitch over;
rem = remaining;
rep = repeat;
RS = right side;
sl = slip;
st(s) = stitch(es);
st st = stocking/ stockinette stitch;
tog = together;
WS = wrong side

Instructions

SOCKS: (Make 2)
With 3.75mm (no. 9/US 5) needles and C, cast on 43 sts.
1st row: K1, (p1, k1) to end.
2nd row: P1, (k1, p1) to end.
Rep these 2 rows once more.
Change to 4mm (no. 8/US 6) needles. Beg with a k row, work 2 rows in st st. Join in M. Cont in st st and patt from chart as foll, stranding yarn not in use loosely across WS of work:
1st row: (RS) Reading from right to left, rep 6 sts of chart to last st, k1.
2nd row: Reading from left to right, p1, rep 6 sts of chart to end.

Cont in this way until 13 rows from chart have been completed. Cut off C. Cont in M only and beg with a p row, work 6 rows st st, ending with a k row.
Next row: K to end to reverse fabric. Beg and ending with a p row, work 35 rows in st st.
Work instep:
Next row: K32, turn and leave rem 11 sts on a holder.
Next row: P21, turn and leave rem 11 sts on another holder.
Work 32 more rows in st st on these 21 sts, ending with a p row (adjust length here if required).
Shape toe:
Next row: K1, sl 1, k1, psso, k to last 3 sts, k2tog, k1.
Next row: P to end.
Rep last 2 rows until 11 sts rem, ending with a p row. Cut off yarn and leave sts on a holder.
Work heel:
Join back leg seam, reversing seam at cuff.

With RS facing, k across rem 22 sts as foll: k10, k2tog, k10. 21 sts. Work 13 rows more in st st, ending with a p row.

Shape heel:

Next row: K13, sl 1, k1, psso, turn, *sl 1, p5, p2tog, turn, sl 1, k5, sl 1, k1, psso, turn, rep from * 5 times more, sl 1, p5, p2tog, turn. 7 sts.

Next row: K7, with RS facing, pick up and k7 sts along side of heel.

Next row: P14, with WS facing, pick up and p7 sts along other side of heel. 21 sts.

Work 32 rows more (or length required) in st st, ending with a p row.

Shape toe:

Next row: K1, sl 1, k1, psso, k to last 3 sts, k2tog, k1.

Next row: P to end.

Rep last 2 rows until 11 sts rem, ending with a p row. Do not cut off yarn.

With RS facing, sl 11 instep toe sts on to spare needle. With RS tog, holding both needles with toe sts in left hand, instep sts in front of heel sts, and points of needles tog, Cast/bind off both pieces tog, taking 1 st from instep tog with 1 st from heel for every st.

 ## Making up

Press according to directions on ball band. Join side seams of foot. Fold back cuff (chart above right), as shown in photograph.

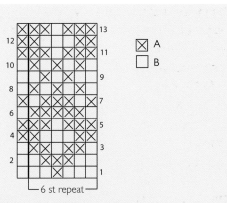

6 st repeat

A
B

Fancy-fringed scarf

With its stunning colour mix and chunky fringes, this is a great scarf to add zing to a plain outfit.

The Yarn
King Cole Magnum Multi Chunky is a practical mix of 75% acrylic with 25% wool. Its thick, loose fibres twist together and knit up very quickly, while the variegated shades provide a fashionable and colourful fabric with the minimum of effort.

Wrap yourself in this colourful scarf that is fast to knit in chunky yarn and a simple rib pattern. Fringes along one long edge, as well as the short ends, add a fashionable twist.

GETTING STARTED

 Quick and easy project, perfect for beginners

Size:
Scarf is 13cm wide x 160cm long (5in x 63in), excluding fringes

How much yarn:
3 x 100g (3½oz) balls of King Cole Magnum Multi Chunky, approx 110m (120 yards) per ball

Needles:
Pair of 10mm (no. 000/US 15) knitting needles

Additional items:
Crochet hook for fringing

Tension/gauge:
10 sts and 12 rows to 10cm (4in) square over rib patt on 10mm (no. 000/US 15) needles
IT IS ESSENTIAL TO WORK TO THE STATED TENSION/GAUGE TO ACHIEVE SUCCESS

What you have to do:
Repeat two rows of rib pattern for length of scarf. Use crochet hook to knot fringes into two short ends and one long end.

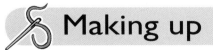 # Instructions

Abbreviations:
cm = centimetre(s); **k** = knit; **p** = purl; **rep** = repeat; **st(s)** = stitch(es);

SCARF:
With 10mm (no. 000/US 15) needles cast on 13 sts.
1st row: K4, (p1, k3) to last st, k1.
2nd row: K2, (p1, k3) to last 3 sts, p1, k2.
Rep these 2 rows to form rib patt until Scarf measures 160cm (63in) long. Cast/bind off in patt.

Making up

Cut yarn into 25cm (10in) lengths for fringes. Taking two strands together each time and using crochet hook, knot four fringes evenly spaced along cast-on and cast/bound-off edges. Then work in same way along one long edge, working a fringe into every 4th row-end.

HOW TO
KNIT A SCARF

1 The scarf has a two-row pattern. Begin the first row of the pattern by knitting the first four stitches, then work a purl one, knit three repeat to the last stitch and knit one.

2 The second row consists of knit two and then the purl one, knit three repeat to the last three stitches. Purl the next stitch and then knit the last two.

3 This simple pattern is repeated until the scarf measures 160cm (63in).

4 Cast/bind off the scarf in pattern, making sure that the cast/bound-off edge is not too tight and the edge of the scarf is flat.

5 To make the fringes, cut 25cm (10in) lengths of yarn and take two strands for each fringe. Starting with the cast/bound-off and cast-on edges, insert the crochet hook through the fabric just above the edge and hook the two strands.

6 Bring the strands and the crochet hook back through the fabric and then take the ends of the strands through the loop formed. Pull the ends to tighten the knot.

7 Space four fringes evenly along the cast/bound-off and cast-on edges and then carry on along one of the long edges, making a fringe in every fourth row end.

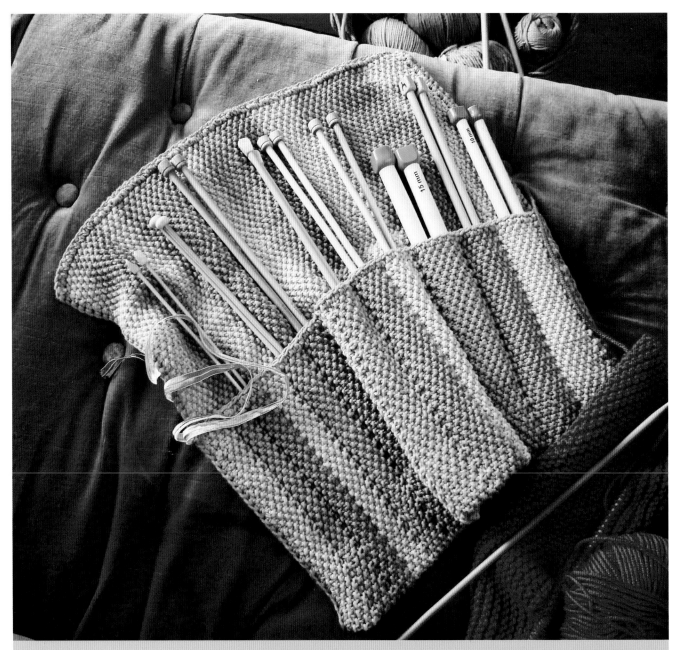

Striped knitting needle case

Knit your own needle case in bold stripes and easy moss/seed stitch.

Be organized with this neat roll-up case for all your knitting needles. The fabric is worked in graduated stripes – from narrow to wide so there is a compartment for each needle size and a felt lining protects the needle points.

The Yarn

Rowan Handknit Cotton is 100% pure cotton yarn in a double knitting (light worsted) weight. It provides good stitch definition for textured patterns such as moss/seed stitch and it is available in a wide range of shades for colourful stripe combinations.

GETTING STARTED

Simple piece of moss/seed-stitch fabric but care is needed with crochet edging and pockets

Size:

Case is 40cm wide x 40cm deep (16in x 16in)

How much yarn:

2 x 50g (2oz) balls of Rowan Handknit Cotton, approx 85m (93 yards) per ball, in each of colours A, B and C

Needles:

Pair of 4mm (no. 8/US 6) knitting needles

Additional items:

4mm (no. 8/US 6) crochet hook
60cm (24in) length of ribbon, 10cm x 40cm (4in x 16in) piece of felt
Sewing needle and thread

Tension/gauge:

20 sts and 32 rows measure 10cm (4in) square over moss/seed st on 4mm (no. 8/US 6) needles
IT IS ESSENTIAL TO WORK TO THE STATED TENSION/GAUGE TO ACHIEVE SUCCESS

What you have to do:

Work in moss/seed stitch in 3-colour stripe pattern. Neaten edges with simple crochet edging. Sew in felt to protect needle points. Sew lines of running stitches to make up pockets for needles. Sew on ribbon tie.

Instructions

Abbreviations:
beg = beginning; **ch** = chain;
cm = centimetre(s); **cont** = continue;
dc = double crochet (US **sc** = single
crochet); **foll** = follows; **k** = knit;
p = purl; **rep** = repeat; **RS** = right
side; **ss** = slip stitch; **st(s)** = stitch(es);
tog = together; **WS** = wrong side

CASE:
With A, cast on 119 sts.
1st row: (RS) K1, *p1, k1, rep from *
to end.
Rep this row to form moss/seed st.
With A, work 5 more rows in moss/
seed st. Cont in moss/seed st and
stripes as foll: 6 rows each B and C; 8
rows each A, B and C; 10 rows each A,
B and C; 12 rows each A, B and C; 14
rows A. With A, Cast/bind off loosely in
moss/seed st.

Making up

Press according to directions on ball band.

CROCHET EDGING:
With 4mm (no. 8/US 6) hook, B and RS of work facing,
insert crochet hook in first st of cast/bound-off edge, 2ch,
1dc (US sc) in each of next 2 sts, *miss 1 st, 1dc (US sc)
in each of next 3 sts, rep from * to end of cast/bound-off
edge, work another 2dc (US sc) in last st to turn corner,
for short side work into row-ends as foll: miss 1 row, 1dc
(US sc) in next row, rep from * to end of short edge, work
another 2dc (US sc) in last row to turn corner, work across
cast-on edge as foll: 1dc (US sc) in each of next 2 sts, *miss
1 st, 1dc (US sc) in each of next 3 sts, rep from * to end of
cast-on edge, work another 2dc (US sc) in last st to turn
corner, for short side, work into row-ends as foll: * miss 1
row, 1dc (US sc) in next row, rep from * to end of short
edge, work 1dc (US sc) more in last row, join with a ss to
top of 2ch. Fasten off.

FELT NEEDLE-POINT PROTECTOR:
Place needle case on a flat surface, with WS facing up and
stripes running vertically with narrow stripes on the left.
Measure 15cm (6in) up from lower edge and sew a line of
tacking/basting sts across the width. Place piece of felt with
its lower edge along this marked line and tack/baste in place
around all sides. Neatly slip stitch the top and lower edges
of the felt to the needle case to secure. Fold up lower edge
of case to form a pocket measuring 20cm (8in) (felt insert
should be folded in half). Make sure top edge of pocket is
level by matching it to a line of moss/seed st 'pips' across
the width. Using a large sharp needle, B and beg at crochet
edge, sew each needle pocket by working running sts
through both thicknesses, matching edge of each stripe and
working through felt at lower edge. Sew side edges tog by
working through crochet sts.
Remove tacking/basting.
Fold ribbon in half and sew securely to narrow stripe edge
of case, level with pockets. Fill with needles, roll up from the
wide-stripe end and use ribbon to close.

HOW TO
WORK A CROCHET EDGING

The edges of the knitting needle case are finished with a simple crochet edging worked in one of the shades of green.

1 With the right side of the fabric facing, insert the crochet hook in the first stitch of the cast/bound-off edge and work two chain stitches, then make one double crochet (US single = sc) into each of the next two stitches. To make a double crochet (US sc): insert the hook through the stitch and catch the yarn with the hook, draw the hook back through the stitch. Wrap the yarn around the hook and draw it through the two loops on the hook. One loop remains on the hook.

2 Miss one stitch and make one double crochet (US sc) in each of the next three stitches.

3 Repeat step 2 to the end of the cast/bound-off edge.

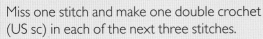

4 To turn the corner, work another two double crochet into the last stitch.

5 On the row end side, miss one row and work one double crochet (US sc) into the next row end.

6 Continue in this way to the end of this side (as shown). To continue the edging, turn the corner by making two double crochet (US sc) into the last stitch and then follow the instructions for the cast-on edge and the final row end side. To finish the edging, make an extra double crochet (US sc) in the last stitch and join it to the first chain with a slip stitch.

Boyfriend sweater

You could knit this for your boyfriend, but then there's the hassle of borrowing it back — so why not just treat yourself?

Warm and cuddly in soft Aran (fisherman) yarn, this V-neck sweater is generously sized for relaxed and casual weekend wear.

Some increasing and decreasing, but mostly in straightforward stocking/stockinette stitch

Size:
86–81[86–91:97–102]cm/
32–34[34–36:38–40]in
109[120:131]cm/43[47¼:51½]in
65[68.5:72]cm/25½[27:28½]in
47[48.5:50]cm/18½[19:19¾]in
Figures in square brackets [ ] refer to larger sizes; where there is only one set of figures, it applies to all sizes

How much yarn:
15[16:17] x 50g (2oz) balls of Debbie Bliss Rialto Aran, approx 80m (87 yards) per ball

Needles:
Pair of 4.5mm (no. 7/US 7) knitting needles
Pair of 5mm (no. 6/US 8) knitting needles

Tension/gauge:
18 sts and 24 rows measure 10cm (4in) square over st st on 5mm (no. 6/US 8) needles

What you have to do:
Work in stocking/stockinette stitch. Leave stitches on a spare needle or stitch holder to work each side of neck separately. Decrease stitches to shape V-neck. Increase stitches to shape sleeves.

The Yarn

With 55% merino wool, Debbie Bliss Rialto Aran is the perfect yarn to achieve stocking/ stockinette stitch that is smooth and even and to create a fabric that feels soft and luxurious. There is a colour palette of fabulous shades, including jewel brights as well as neutrals and pastels, to suit every taste.

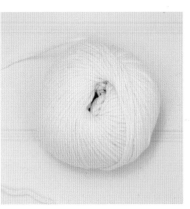

Abbreviations:

alt = alternate;
beg = beginning;
cont = continue;
dec = decrease;
foll = following;
inc = increase(ing);
k = knit; **p** = purl;
rem = remain(ing);
RS = right side;
st(s) = stitch(es);
st st = stocking/
stockinette stitch;
tbl = through back
of loops;
k2tog = knit 2 stitches
together

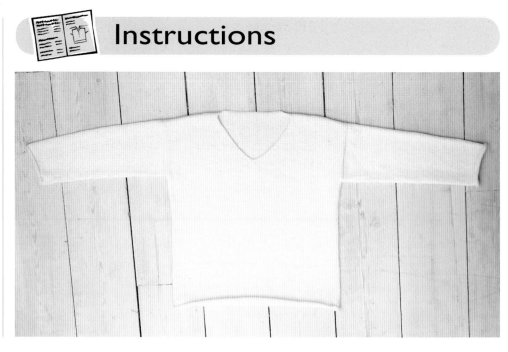

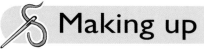

Instructions

BACK:

With 4.5mm (no. 7/US 7) needles cast on 100[110:120] sts. Beg with a k row, work 4 rows in st st. Change to 5mm (no. 6/US 8) needles.* Work another 152[160:168] rows in st st, ending with a p row.

Shape shoulders:

Cast/bind off 11[12:13] sts at beg of next 6 rows. Cast/bind off rem 34[38:42] sts.

FRONT:

Work as Back to *. Work another 118[122:126] rows in st st, ending with a p row.

Shape neck:

Next row: K47[52:57], k2tog, k1, turn and leave rem sts on a spare needle or stitch holder.

Cont on these 49[54:59] sts for left front. P 1 row.

Dec 1 st at neck edge on next and every foll alt row to 33[36:39] sts, ending with a p row.

Shape shoulder:

Cast/bind off 11[12:13] sts at beg of next and foll alt row. Work 1 row. Cast/bind off rem 11[12:13] sts.

With RS of work facing, rejoin yarn to sts on spare needle or stitch holder, k1, k2tog tbl, k to end. Work to match first side of neck, reversing shapings.

Sleeves: (Make 2)

With 4.5mm (no. 7/US 7) needles cast on 52[58:64] sts. Beg with a k row, work 4 rows in st st. Change to 5mm (no. 6/US 8) needles. Cont in st st, inc 1 st at each end of next and every foll 12th row until there are 70[76:82] sts. Work 11[15:19] rows straight, ending with a p row. Cast/bind off.

Making up

Press the pieces carefully using a warm iron over a clean cloth. Do not press the lower edges of the back, front and sleeves as these should be allowed to roll up.

Joining the seams:

Using backstitch, join shoulder seams. Mark position of underarms about 19[21:23]cm/7½[8¼:9]in down from shoulders on back and front. Matching the centre of top edges of sleeves to shoulder seams, sew in sleeves between markers. Join side and sleeve seams.

HOW TO
USE A STITCH HOLDER

Stitch holders are a useful tool for the knitter and are constructed like a giant safety pin. They come in a variety of lengths and you can select the holder according to the number of stitches that you need to store on it.

3 Open the stitch holder and slide the stitches, one by one, onto the left-hand needle. Again, be careful not to twist the stitches.

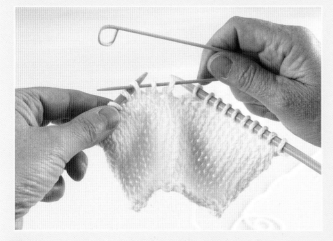

1 Knit to the instructed point in the row. Open the stitch holder and slide the needle end under each stitch on the left-hand needle. Keeping the stitches the right way around, take them onto the holder. Clip the holder shut.

4 Join in the yarn on the right-hand edge and knit the remaining stitches for the instructed length.

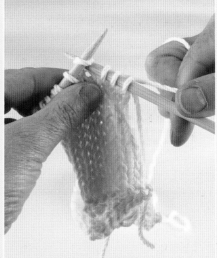

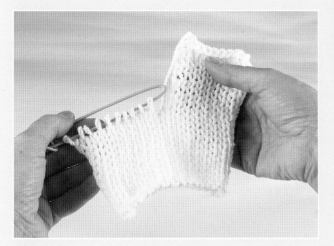

2 Continue knitting the stitches remaining on the right-hand needle for the instructed length and then cast/bind off.

5 This is the effect created by working two sets of stitches separately and in this pattern it is used to create the v-neck.

Featherweight throw

Light as a feather, this throw is made for snuggling down and watching old movies.

Worked with brushed yarn on big needles, this gorgeous throw is unbelievably light and airy. Made up of identical squares, it has a novel construction – the cast-on edge forms the entire outer edge of the square, which is then shaped inward.

The Yarn

Rowan Kid Classic contains 70% acrylic, 22% and 8% Polyamide. Worked on big needles, it makes lightweight fabrics with a luxurious appearance. There are plenty of colours to choose from in muted, subtle shades. You can hand wash this yarn carefully, and dry cleaning is also recommended.

GETTING STARTED

 Easy once you have made one square as all the rest are the same

Size:

Throw measures 108cm x 144cm (42½in x 57in), excluding fringe

How much yarn:

8 x 50g (2oz) balls of Rowan Kid Classic, approx 140m (153 yards) per ball

Needles:

Pair of 6mm (no. 4/US 10) knitting needles

Additional items:

Crochet hook for tassels

Tension/gauge:

Each square measures approximately 18cm (7in) square; 12 sts and 28 rows measure 10cm (4in) square over garter st worked on 6mm (no. 4/US 10) needles IT IS ESSENTIAL TO WORK TO THE STATED TENSION/ GAUGE TO ACHIEVE SUCCESS

What you have to do:

Cast on using 2-needle method for a loose edge. Work from outer edge in to centre, first in garter stitch, then in stocking/stockinette stitch. Use decorative decreasing to form 45-degree angles so shaping into square. Draw up remaining stitches at centre of square, then sew side edges to form last 'angle'. Sew squares together through the looped cast-on edges. Knot a fringe into both short ends of throw.

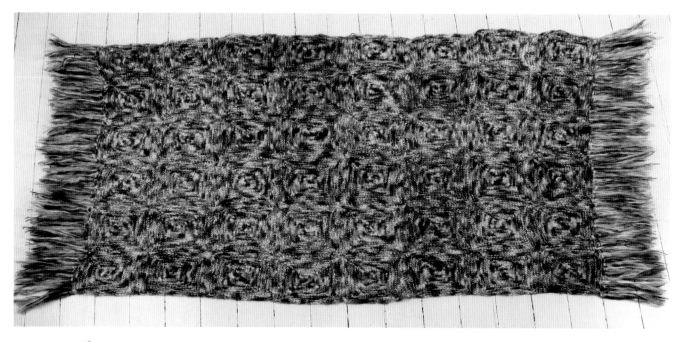

 # Instructions

Abbreviations:

alt = alternate; **cm** = centimetre(s); **cont** = continue; **dec** = decrease(ing); **foll** = following; **k** = knit; **p** = purl; **psso** = pass slipped stitch over; **rem** = remain; **sl** = slip; **st(s)** = stitch(es); **tbl** = through back of loops; **tog** = together; **WS** = wrong side

TO MAKE A SQUARE:

(Make 48 squares in total)

Cast on 87 sts using the 2-needle method to obtain a loose edge and leaving about 45cm (18in) of yarn free at start to use for sewing up.

1st and 4 foll alt rows: (WS) K to end. (Do not knit into back of sts on 1st row because the 'loop' edge will help sewing up and becomes a feature in the finished throw.)

2nd row: K1, k2tog tbl, (k18, sl 1, k2tog, psso) 3 times, k18, k2tog, k1. 79 sts.

4th row: K1, k2tog tbl, (k16, sl 1, k2tog, psso) 3 times, k16, k2tog, k1. 71 sts.

6th row: K1, k2tog tbl, (k14, sl 1, k2tog, psso) 3 times, k14, k2tog, k1. 63 sts.

8th row: K1, k2tog tbl, (k12, sl 1, k2tog, psso) 3 times, k12, k2tog, k1. 55 sts.

10th row: K1, k2tog tbl, (k10, sl 1, k2tog, psso) 3 times, k10, k2tog, k1. 47 sts.

11th and every foll alt row: P to end.

Cont in this way, dec 8 sts on next and every k row, until 15 sts rem, ending with a dec row. Cut off yarn, leaving about 18cm (7in) free. Thread cut end through rem sts, draw up and fasten off. Use end of yarn to join side edges using a backstitch seam.

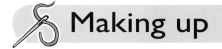

Making up

Do not press.
Use a loose over-sewing st to link the cast-on loops tog, sewing squares tog in 8 rows with 6 squares in each row.
Fringe: Cut remaining yarn into 38cm (15in) lengths. Taking 4 strands tog for each tassel, fringe the two short ends, using a crochet hook to work a tassel into alternate loops along short edges.

Checkered wrap

This is the ultimate holiday accessory – a cosy lightweight shawl for wrapping up and chilling out.

This generously sized cosy wrap with large mosaic-patterned checks is worked in a beautiful natural yarn containing alpaca.

GETTING STARTED

Straight piece of fabric and coloured pattern is easier to work than it looks

Size:
Wrap is approximately 53cm wide x 150cm long (21in x 59in), excluding fringe

How much yarn:
6 x 50g (2oz) balls of Sirdar Peru Naturals, approx 90m (99 yards) per ball, in dark colour D
5 balls in light colour L

Needles:
Pair of 6.5mm (no. 3/US 10½) knitting needles

Additional items:
Crochet hook for fringing

Tension/gauge:
15 sts and 28 rows measure 10cm (4in) square over patt on 6.5mm (no. 3/US 10½) needles
IT IS ESSENTIAL TO WORK TO THE STATED TENSION/GAUGE TO ACHIEVE SUCCESS

What you have to do:
Work throughout in slip stitch pattern. Keep two stitches in garter stitch at each end of rows for side borders. Use separate small ball of yarn for left border and twist yarns together when changing colour. Add fringes to ends using a crochet hook.

The Yarn
Sirdar Peru Naturals contains 64% wool, 31% acrylic and 5% alpaca. It is a chunky weight that can be handwashed at a cool temperature. There is a small range of colours that are all subtly shaded for a natural effect.

Abbreviations:
cm = centimetre(s);
cont = continue;
foll = follows;
k = knit;
p = purl;
patt = pattern;
rep = repeat;
RS = right side;
sl = slip;
st(s) = stitch(es);
st st = stocking/
stockinette stitch;
ytb = yarn to back;
ytf = yarn to front

Instructions

WRAP:

Note: To avoid twisting always slip sts purlwise.
Wind off approximately one third of a ball of D for left border.
With D, cast on 79 sts. Cont in patt as foll, twisting yarns tog when changing colour at borders on L rows to avoid a hole:

1st row: (RS) With D, k to end.

2nd row: With D, k2, p to last 2 sts, k2.

3rd row: With D, k2 for border; with L, *k15, (sl 1, k1) 7 times, sl 1*, rep from * to *, k15, with small ball of D, k2 for border.

4th row: With D, k2, ytf, with L, *p15, (sl 1, ytb, k1, ytf) 7 times, sl 1*, rep from * to *, p15 L, with D, k2.

5th row: With D, k2, *(sl 1, k1) 7 times, sl 1, k15*, rep from * to *, (sl 1, k1) 7 times, sl 1, k2.

6th row: With D, k2, ytf, *(sl 1, ytb, k1, ytf) 7 times, sl 1, p15*, rep from * to * (sl 1, ytb, k1, ytf) 7 times, sl 1, k2.

7th–28th rows: Rep 3rd–6th rows 5 times, then 3rd and 4th rows again.

29th and 30th rows: As 1st and 2nd rows.

31st row: With D, k2, with L, *(sl 1, k1) 7 times, sl 1, k15*, rep from * to *, (sl 1, k1) 7 times, sl 1, with D, k2.

32nd row: With D, k2, ytf, with L, *(sl 1, ytb, k1, ytf) 7 times, sl 1, p15*, rep from * to *, (sl 1, ytb, k1, ytf) 7 times, sl 1, with D, k2.

33rd row: With D, k2, *k15, (sl 1, k1) 7 times, sl 1*, rep from * to *, k17.

34th row: With D, k2, *p15, (sl 1, ytb, k1, ytf) 7 times, sl 1*, rep from * to *, p15, k2.

35th–56th rows: Rep 31st–34th rows 5 times more, then work 31st and 32nd rows again.

These 56 rows form patt. Rep them 6 times more, then work 1st–29th rows again. With D, Cast/bind off as 30th row.

Fringe:

With crochet hook and using 6 strands of yarn 27cm (10½in) long each time, work fringing along cast/bound-on and cast-off edges. Begin and end in each corner and work 4 fringes in one colour for each 10cm (4in) square of patt, alternating colours for each square.

Magazine basket

Have some fun with string and yarn when you knit this chunky, box-shaped basket.

Lined with fabric and strengthened, this rustic-looking magazine basket with slot handles is quick to knit in a combination of denim-style yarn and string.

GETTING STARTED

Easy knitted pieces but construction involves some hand-sewing

Size:
Basket is 36cm high x 38cm wide x 11cm deep
(14¼in x 15in x 4½in)

How much yarn:
4 x 100g (3½oz) balls of Sirdar Denim Ultra,
approx 75m (82 yards) per ball
4 x 50g (2oz) reels of parcel string

Needles:
Pair of 10mm (no. 000/US 15) knitting needles

Additional items:
1m (1 yard) of heavyweight lining fabric
Matching sewing thread and needle
Two 34cm x 25cm (13½in x 10in) rectangles
corrugated cardboard; three 34cm x 10cm (13½in
x 4in) strips corrugated cardboard

Tension/gauge:
8.5 sts and 13 rows measure 10cm (4in) square
over st st using yarn and string together
IT IS ESSENTIAL TO WORK TO THE STATED
TENSION/GAUGE TO ACHIEVE SUCCESS

What you have to do:
Work main fabric in stocking/stockinette stitch and
garter stitch. Make a cast/bound-off 'buttonhole-style'
opening in each side panel for slot handles. Line knitted
pieces with fabric and insert cardboard for stiffening.

The Yarn
Sirdar Denim
Ultra contains 60%
acrylic, 25% cotton
and 15% wool. It
is an extra-chunky,
hard-wearing
yarn in variegated
colourways that
resemble the
faded appearance of denim fabric. For extra strength
and natural good looks, we have knitted ordinary
parcel string together with Denim Ultra.

Abbreviations:

beg = beginning;
cm = centimetre(s);
g st = garter stitch (every row knit);
k = knit;
RS = right side;
st(s) = stitch(es);
st st = stocking/ stockinette stitch

Note: Work with 1 strand each of Denim Ultra and string together throughout.

Instructions

HOW TO
USE YARN AND STRING

1 Using string with yarn adds another dimension to the texture of the finished fabric. Use a spool of parcel string alongside the ball of yarn.

2 Holding the yarn and string together, cast on in the usual way.

3 As you knit, make sure that the string and yarn are tensioned the same way through the fingers of your right hand. In this way, the two will sit neatly side by side in each stitch.

MAIN PANELS: (Make 2)

Cast on 32 sts. Beg with a k row, work 35 rows in st st, ending with a k row. Now work 5 rows in g st. Make slot for handle:

Next row: (RS) K10, cast/bind off next 12 sts, k to end.

Next row: K to end, casting on 12 sts over those cast/bound off in previous row. Work 6 more rows in g st. Cast/bind off.

SIDE PANELS: (Make 2)

Cast on 12 sts. Beg with a k row, work 35 rows in st st, ending with a k row. Now work 13 rows in g st. Cast/bind off.

BASE:

Cast on 32 sts. Beg with a k row, work 16 rows in st st. Cast/bind off.

 ## Making up

Using panels and base as templates, cut linings from fabric. Press under 1cm (⅜in) turnings around all edges. Place one lining strip on WS of a knitted side panel, leaving 1cm (⅜in) free all around edges and slip stitch in place around three sides, leaving top edge (g st section) open. Insert cardboard strip and close opening. Repeat for other side panel and insert cardboard into knitted base in a similar way.

Place one lining square on WS of a knitted main panel, leaving 1cm (⅜in) free all around edges, and slip stitch in place around three sides, leaving bottom (st st section open). Carefully cut a slot in the lining to match the handle opening and cut into the corners. Fold lining around handle to WS to neaten and slip stitch in place around opening. Insert cardboard into open lower edge and slip stitch lining closed. Pushing cardboard as close to the lower edge as possible, work a neat seam joining lining to knitting at top edge of cardboard, about 4cm (1½in) down from handle opening. Repeat for other main panel.

With RS of one side panel and base together, join seam at lower edge with backstitch. Repeat for other side panel. Working on RS, carefully pin sides and base of basket to main panels, aligning top edges and corners. Sew together using mattress stitch.

Skinny Fair Isle scarf

Combine Fair Isle techniques with straightforward stocking/ stockinette stitch for this stylish scarf.

Worked in stocking/stockinette stitch with moss/seed stitch edgings, this fine wool scarf has panels of distinctive graphic Fair Isle patterns at each end.

GETTING STARTED

Fair Isle techniques for patterned panels will take some practice

Size:
Scarf is 20cm wide x 148.5cm long (8in x 58½in)

How much yarn:
3 x 50g (2oz) balls of Debbie Bliss Rialto 4-ply, approx 180m (197 yards) per ball, in main colour A
1 ball in each of four contrast colours B, C, D and E

Needles:
Pair of 3.25mm (no. 10/US 3) knitting needles

Tension/gauge:
28 sts and 36 rows measure 10cm (4in) square over st st on 3.25mm (no. 10/US 3) needles
IT IS ESSENTIAL TO WORK TO THE STATED TENSION/GAUGE TO ACHIEVE SUCCESS

What you have to do:
Work borders in moss/seed stitch and main fabric in stocking/stockinette stitch. At each end of scarf work Fair Isle pattern panel from a chart. Use Fair Isle techniques of stranding yarn not in use loosely across wrong side of work.

The Yarn
Debbie Bliss Rialto 4-ply is 100% extra fine merino wool. It gives good stitch definition for stocking/stockinette stitch fabrics and can be machine washed at a low temperature. There are plenty of beautiful contemporary shades to choose from for original colour work.

Instructions

SCARF:

With B, cast on 57 sts.

1st row: K1, (p1, k1) to end.

Rep this row to form moss/seed st. Work 3 more rows in moss/seed st.

Change to A and cont as foll:

1st row: (RS) Moss/seed st 3, k to last 3 sts, moss/seed st 3.

2nd row: Moss/seed st 3, p to last 3 sts, moss/seed st 3.

Cont in st st with 3 sts in moss/seed st at each end as set, work 2 more rows in A, 4 rows in B and 4 rows in A.

Place chart 1:

Next row: (RS) Moss/seed st 3 A, k across 51 sts of chart 1 stranding yarn not in use loosely across WS of work, moss/seed st 3 A.

Next row: Moss/seed st 3 A, p across 51 sts of 1st row of chart 1, moss/seed st 3 A.

Keeping edge sts correct, cont in st st and Fair Isle patt from chart 1 until

25 rows have been completed.

Now cont in A only until work measures 137cm (54in) from beg, ending with a WS row.

Place chart 2:

Next row: (RS) Moss/seed st 3 A, k across 51 sts of 1st row of chart 2 stranding yarn not in use loosely across WS of work, moss/seed st 3 A.

Next row: Moss/seed st 3 A, p across 51 sts of 2nd row of chart 2, moss/seed st 3 A.

Keeping edge sts correct, cont in st st and Fair Isle patt from chart 2 until 25 rows have been completed.

Cont in A only, work 3 rows, then 4 rows in B and 4 rows in A. Cut off A. With B, work 4 rows in moss/seed st. Cast/bind off in moss/seed st.

Making up

Sew in all ends. Press lightly according to directions on ball band.

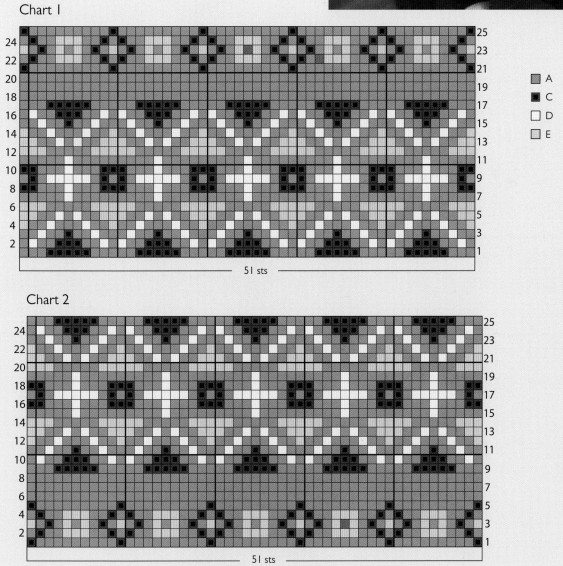

Chart 1

51 sts

A
C
D
E

Chart 2

51 sts

Aran throw

Classic cable design and a soft chunky yarn make this a wonderful throw to keep you snug on chilly evenings.

A hand-knitted throw is a priceless treasure, especially this one as it is richly textured with cable patterns. Knitting it in three separate panels makes it easy to handle.

GETTING STARTED

Good practice for working cables as each panel of this throw is just a straight strip with no shaping involved

Size:
Throw measures 125cm x 154cm (49in x 60½in)

How much yarn:
31 x 50g (2oz) balls of Sirdar Sublime Cashmere Merino Silk Aran, approx 86m (94 yards) per ball

Needles:
Pair of 4mm (no. 8/US 6) knitting needles
Pair of 5mm (no. 6/US 8) knitting needles
Cable needle

Tension/gauge:
18 sts and 24 rows to 10cm (4in) square over st st worked on 5mm (no. 6/US 8) needles
IT IS ESSENTIAL TO WORK TO THE STATED TENSION/ GAUGE TO ACHIEVE SUCCESS

What you have to do:
Work three separate vertical patterned panels. Work in garter stitch (every row knit) for borders. Work cables of varying complexity. Sew the panels together to form throw.

The Yarn
Sirdar Sublime Cashmere Merino Silk Aran is a luxurious blend of 75% extra-fine merino wool with 20% silk and 5% cashmere. It is incredibly soft and comes in ten beautiful subtle shades for making irresistible textured knits.

Abbreviations:

cm = centimetre(s);
cn = cable needle;
cont = continue;
dec = decrease;
foll = follows;
g st = garter stitch (every row knit);
inc = increase;
k = knit;
k1b = knit into back of stitch;
m1 = make 1 stitch by picking up horizontal strand lying between needles and knitting into back of it;
p = purl; **patt** = pattern;
RS = right side; **sl** = slip;
st(s) = stitch(es);
st st = stocking/ stockinette stitch;
tog = together;
WS = wrong side
BC = sl 1 st on to cn and leave at back of work, k2, then p1 from cn
FC = sl 2 sts on to cn and leave at front of work, p1, then k2 from cn
C3B = sl 1 st on to cn and leave at back of work, k2, then k1 from cn
C3F = sl 2 sts on to cn and leave at front of work, k1, then k2 from cn
C4 = sl 2 sts on to cn and leave at back of work, k2, then k2 from cn
C8B = sl 4 sts on to cn and leave at back of work, k4, then k4 from cn
C8F = sl 4 sts on to cn and leave at front of work, k4, then k4 from cn

 # Instructions

THROW:
Note: Throw is made up of three panels:
PANEL ONE – to the right of centre panel as you look at it
PANEL TWO – centre panel
PANEL THREE – to the left of centre panel as you look at it

Pattern A: (Worked over 12 sts)
1st row: (WS) k1, p10, k1.
2nd row: P4, C4, p4.
3rd row: K4, p4, k4.
4th row: P3, C3B, C3F, p3.
5th row: K3, p6, k3.
6th row: P2, C3B, k2, C3F, p2.
7th row: K2, p8, k2.
8th row: P1, C3B, k4, C3F, p1.
These 8 rows form patt and are repeated throughout.

Pattern B: (Worked over 20 sts)
1st row: (WS) K3, p2, k3, p4, k3, p2, k3.
2nd row: (P2, BC) twice, (FC, p2) twice.
3rd and every foll WS row: K all k sts and p all p sts.
4th row: P1, (BC, p2) twice, FC, p2, FC, p1.
6th row: (BC, p2) twice, (p2, FC) twice.
8th row: (FC, p2) twice, (p2, BC) twice.
10th row: P1, (FC, p2) twice, BC, p2, BC, p1.
12th row: (P2, FC) twice, (BC, p2) twice. These 12 rows form patt and are repeated throughout.

PANEL ONE:
With 4mm (no. 8/US 6) needles cast on 75 sts. Work 10 rows in g st.
Inc row: (RS) K23, *m1, k3, m1, k2, rep from * 6 times more, m1, k17. 90 sts.
Change to 5mm (no. 6/US 8) needles. Cont in patt as foll:
1st, 3rd and 5th rows: (WS) P18, k2, p2, (k2, p8, k2, p2) 3 times, k2, p18, k6.
2nd and 4th rows: K24, p2, k2, (p2, k8, p2, k2) 3 times, p2, k18.

6th row: K24, p2, k2, (p2, C8B, p2, k2) 3 times, p2, k18.
7th, 9th and 11th rows: As 1st row.
8th, 10th and 12th rows: As 2nd row. These 12 rows form patt and are repeated throughout. Rep them 29 times more.
Change to 4mm (no. 8/US 6) needles.
Dec row: (WS) K17, *k2tog, k2, k2tog, k1, rep from * 6 times more, k2tog, k22. 75 sts.
Work 9 rows in g st. Cast/bind off fairly loosely.

PANEL TWO:
With 4mm (no. 8/US 6) needles cast on 79 sts. Work 10 rows in g st.
Inc row: (RS) K1, *m1, k2, rep from * 37 times more, m1, k2. 118 sts.
Change to 5mm (no. 6/US 8) needles. Cont in patt as foll:
1st row: (WS) K1, p1, *work 1st row from Patt A over next 12 sts, p1, work 1st row from Patt B over next 20 sts, p1, rep from * 3 times in all, work 1st row from Patt A over next 12 sts, p1, k1.
2nd row: K1, k1b, *work 2nd row from Patt A over next 12 sts, k1b, work 2nd row from Patt B over next 20 sts, k1b, rep from * 3 times in all, work 2nd row from Patt A over next 12 sts, k1b, k1.
3rd row: K1, p1, *work 3rd row from Patt A over next 12 sts, p1, work 3rd row from Patt B over next 20 sts, p1, rep from * 3 times in all, work 3rd row from Patt A over next 12 sts, p1, k1.
4th row: K1, k1b, *work 4th row from Patt A over next 12 sts, k1b, work 4th row from Patt B over next 20 sts, k1b, rep from * 3 times in all, work 4th row from Patt A over next 12 sts, k1b, k1.
Cont in patt as set until Patt B has been worked 30 times in all.
Change to 4mm (no. 8/US 6) needles.
Dec row: (WS) K1, *k2tog, k1, rep from

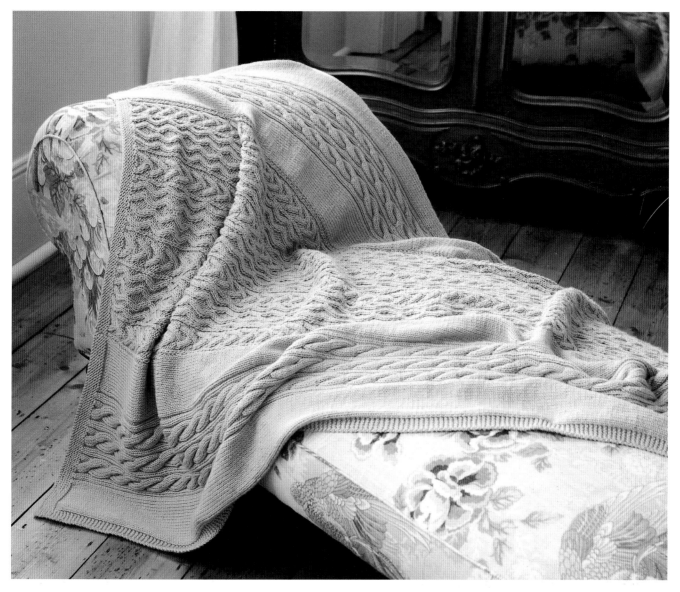

* to end. 79 sts. Work 9 rows in g st. Cast/bind off fairly loosely.

PANEL THREE:

With 4mm (no. 8/US 6) needles cast on 75 sts. Work 10 rows in g st.

Inc row: (RS) K17, *m1, k3, m1, k2, rep from * 6 times more, m1, k23. 90 sts.

Change to 5mm (no. 6/US 8) needles. Cont in patt as foll:

1st, 3rd and 5th rows: (WS) K6, p18, k2, p2, (k2, p8, k2, p2) 3 times, k2, p18.

2nd and 4th rows: K18, p2, k2, (p2, k8, p2, k2) 3 times, p2, k24.

6th row: K18, p2, k2, (p2, C8F, p2, k2) 3 times, p2, k24.

7th, 9th and 11th rows: As 1st row.

8th, 10th and 12th rows: As 2nd row.

These 12 rows form patt and are repeated throughout. Rep them 29 times more.

Change to 4mm (no. 8/US 6) needles.

Dec row: (WS) K22, *k2tog, k2, k2tog, k1, rep from * 6 times more, k2tog, k17. 75 sts.

Work 9 rows in g st. Cast/bind off fairly loosely.

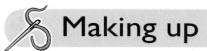 Making up

Press lightly according to instructions on ball band. Sew panels together neatly. Press seams lightly.

Checked neck wrap

Create a dramatic look with this graphic patterned and coloured wrap secured with large buttons.

For a more stylish version of a scarf, try this neck wrap instead. Worked in a dogstooth check pattern with colourful fringing, it wraps over and buttons at the front.

GETTING STARTED

 Slip-stitch checks are easier than intarsia as you only work rows with one colour at a time

Size:
Wrap is approximately 17cm wide x 90cm long (6¾in x 35½in), excluding fringe

How much yarn:
1 x 100g (3½oz), ball of King Cole Magnum Chunky, approx 110m (120 yards) per ball, in each of three colours A – charcoal, B – white and C – rouge

Needles:
Pair of 6mm (no. 4/US 10) knitting needles

Additional items:
Crochet hook for fringing
2 large buttons
Large press stud (popper snap)

Tension/gauge:
11 sts and 26 rows measure 10cm (4in) square over patt on 6mm (no. 4/US 10) needles
IT IS ESSENTIAL TO WORK TO THE STATED TENSION/ GAUGE TO ACHIEVE SUCCESS

What you have to do:
Work integral borders in garter stitch with main colour. Use two colours to work slip-stitch check pattern. Make double crochet (US single crochet) buttonhole edging on one short edge. Add fringe in third colour along lower long edge.

The Yarn
King Cole Magnum Chunky contains 75% premium acrylic and 25% wool. It is a hardwearing yarn that combines the practicalities of manmade fibres with the good looks of wool and there are plenty of traditional and contemporary colours to choose from.

Abbreviations:

Abbreviations:
ch = chain;
cm = centimetre(s);
cont = continue;
dc = double crochet (US
sc = single crochet);
foll = follows;
k = knit;
p = purl;
patt = pattern;
rep = repeat;
RS = right side;
sl = slip purlwise;
st(s) = stitch(es);
WS = wrong side;
ytb = yarn to back;
ytf = yarn to front

Instructions

NECK WRAP:

With A, cast on 21 sts. K 2 rows. Cont in check patt with border in A as foll:

1st row: (RS) Sl 2, with B, (k2, sl 1) to last 4 sts, k2, turn.

2nd row: Ytb, with B, k to last 2 sts, ytf, sl last 2 sts, turn.

3rd row: With A, k2, (sl 1, k2) to last 4 sts, sl 1, k3.

4th row: With A, k to end across all sts. These 4 rows form patt. Rep them 56 times more, then work 1st and 2nd rows again. Cut off B.

With A, k 2 rows. Cast/bind off but do not cut off yarn.

Buttonhole edging:

With crochet hook, A and WS of work facing, work along cast/bound-off edge as foll: 1ch, 1dc (US sc) in each of next 3 sts, 3ch, miss next 3 sts, 1dc (US sc) in each of next 9 sts, 3ch, miss next 3 sts, 1dc (US sc) in each of last 3 sts. Fasten off.

Making up

Overlap wrap right over left, with buttonhole edge on top, to form a V at centre front. Sew on buttons on side border of underside, and sew press stud (popper snap) near top of V.

Cut C in 18cm (7in) lengths. Taking 3 strands together each time and using crochet hook, work fringing along lower long edge, working a fringe in both corners and approximately every 4 rows of border.

Funky Fair Isle tea cosy

Afternoon tea takes on a fun look with this amazing patterned cosy.

Brighten up the tea table with this cheery pompom-trimmed cosy in multi-coloured stripes and bands of Fair Isle patterns.

The Yarn
Sublime Extra Fine Merino Wool DK is 100% wool. It is a luxuriously smooth yarn that produces clear stitch definition. There is a large palette of subtle shades to choose from for interesting stripe patterns.

 This design is an easy way to practise simple Fair Isle techniques

Size:
To fit an average 4–6 cup ceramic teapot
Tea cosy is approximately 22cm wide x 20cm high (8½in x 8in)

How much yarn:
1 x 50g (2oz) ball of Sublime Extra Fine Merino Wool DK, approx 116m (127 yards) per ball, in each of six colours A – purple, B – raspberry, C – blue, D – pink, E – teal and F – green

Needles:
Pair of 3.25mm (no. 10/US 3) knitting needles
Pair of 4mm (no. 8/US 6) knitting needles
Pair of 3.25mm (no. 10/US 3) double-pointed needles

Additional items:
Pompom maker or stiff cardboard

Tension/gauge:
22 sts and 28 rows measure 10cm (4in) square over st st on 4mm (no. 8/US 6) needles
IT IS ESSENTIAL TO WORK TO THE STATED TENSION/ GAUGE TO ACHIEVE SUCCESS

What you have to do:
Work lower edge of cosy in moss/seed stitch. Work main fabric in stocking/stockinette stitch and multicoloured stripes. Work bands of Fair Isle patterns in some stripes. Embellish finished fabric with embroidery. Make pompoms to decorate top of cosy.

Abbreviations:

beg = beginning
cm = centimetre(s)
cont = continue
dec = decrease
foll = follows
k = knit;
p = purl
patt = pattern
rep = repeat
RS = right side
st(s) = stitch(es)
st st = stocking/
stockinette stitch
tbl = through back of
loop
tog = together
WS = wrong side

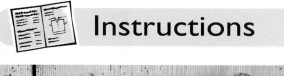

Instructions

FRONT:

With 3.25mm (no. 10/US 3) needles and A, cast on 47 sts.

1st row: P1, (k1, p1) to end.

Rep this row to form moss/seed st. Work 3 more rows in moss/seed st.

Change to 4mm (no. 8/US 6) needles. Beg with a k row, cont in st st and stripes of 2 rows each of B and C.

Cont in st st and patt from chart as foll:

1st row: (RS) Reading chart from right to left, k across 47 sts of 1st row of chart.

2nd row: Reading chart from left to right, p across 47 sts of 2nd row of chart.

Stranding yarn not in use loosely across WS of work, cont in patt from chart until 26 rows have been completed.

Cont in st st and stripes of 2 rows each of E and D. Change to B and cont as foll:

1st dec row: K5, (k2tog, k10) 3 times, k2tog, k4. 43 sts. Beg with a p row, work 3 rows in st st.

2nd dec row: K4, (k2tog, k9) 3 times, k2tog, k4. 39 sts. P 1 row. Cut off B and join in F.

3rd dec row: With F, k4, (k2tog, k8) 3 times, k2tog, k3. 35 sts. P 1 row. Cut off F and join in A.

4th dec row: With A, k3, (k2tog, k7) 3 times, k2tog, k3. 31 sts. P 1 row. Cut off A and join in C.

5th dec row: With C, k3, (k2tog, k6) 3 times, k2tog, k2.

27 sts. P 1 row. Cut off C and join in E.

6th dec row: With E, k2, (k2tog, k5) 3 times, k2tog, k2. 23 sts. P 1 row. Cut off E and join in D.

7th dec row: With D, k2, (k2tog, k4) 3 times, k2tog, k1. 19 sts. P 1 row. Cut off D and join in B.

8th dec row: With B, k1, (k2tog, k3) 3 times, k2tog, k1. 15 sts. P 1 row. Cut off B and join in F.

9th dec row: With F, k1, (k2tog, k2) 3 times, k2tog. 11 sts. P 1 row. Cast/bind off.

BACK:

Work as given for Front.

LOOP:

With 3.25mm (no.10/US 3) double-pointed needles and A, cast on 4 sts. K 1 row.

Next row: *Without turning work and RS facing, slide sts to other end of needle and, pulling yarn from left-hand side of sts to the right tightly across back, k1 tbl, k3. *Rep from * to *, remembering to pull yarn tightly across back and always working a k row, until cord measures 10cm (4in). Cast/bind off.

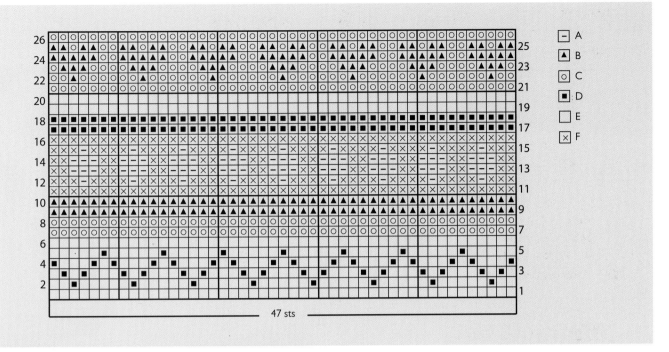

Legend:
- – A
- ▲ B
- ○ C
- ■ D
- □ E
- ☒ F

47 sts

🧵 Making up

Darn in ends of yarn neatly.

With F, embroider French knots in between zig-zags of first Fair Isle band. With A, embroider large cross sts on band in yarn B as shown in photograph (left).

Join side seams as foll: from bottom edge up for approximately 6cm (2½in) on right-hand side, leave about 10cm (4in) open for teapot handle, then join above opening and across top, catching in folded over cord loop. On left-hand side, sew up approximately 6cm (2½in) from bottom edge, leave about 6cm (2½in) open for teapot spout, then sew from above opening to spout.

Using all 6 yarns tog, make 3 pompoms about 4cm (1½in) in diameter. Then make one pompom in each of the following 3 colours: A, B and F. Sew pompoms to top of cosy, around loop, alternating solid and multicolours.

Repeating flower cushion

Four colours are interchanged, almost like an art print, to create this clever cover.

A study in stocking/stockinette stitch and colourful intarsia, this cushion/ pillow has a stylized flower motif in each quarter and a buttoned centre back opening. It will look great in a contemporary setting.

GETTING STARTED

 Although basic fabric is stocking/ stockinette stitch, working colour pattern from a chart requires skill for a neat finish

Size:
Cushion/pillow is 46cm x 46cm (18in x 18in)

How much yarn:
2 x 50g (2oz) balls of Sublime Extra Fine Merino Wool DK, approx 116m (127 yards) per ball, in each of four colours A, B, C and D

Needles:
Pair of 4mm (no. 8/US 6) knitting needles

Additional items:
4 buttons, 46cm (18in) square cushion pad/pillow form

Tension/gauge:
22 sts and 28 rows measure 10cm (4in) square over st st on 4mm (no. 8/US 6) needles
IT IS ESSENTIAL TO WORK TO THE STATED TENSION/GAUGE TO ACHIEVE SUCCESS

What you have to do:
Cast on with two colours for coloured background squares. Work in stocking/stockinette stitch, using intarsia technique of twisting yarns together at back of work when changing colour. Follow chart to work intarsia flower pattern on front. Use small, separate balls of yarn for each area of colour; do not carry yarn across back of work. Work back in two halves (without flowers), making moss/seed-stitch borders for button opening.

The Yarn
Sublime Extra Fine Merino Wool DK is 100% merino wool spun in Italy. It is a luxuriously smooth yarn that gives good stitch definition and there are 25 beautiful subtle and more colourful shades to choose from.

Instructions

Abbreviations:
beg = beginning; **cm** = centimetre(s); **cont** = continue; **foll** = follows; **k** = knit; **p** = purl; **patt** = pattern; rep = repeat; **RS** = right side; **st(s)** = stitch(es); **st st** = stocking/stockinette stitch; **tog** = together; **WS** = wrong side; **yo** = yarn over or round needle to make a stitch

FRONT:
With B, cast on 51 sts, then on to same needle cast on another 51 sts with A. 102 sts. Twisting yarns tog on WS of work when changing colour to avoid a hole forming, cont as foll:
1st row: (RS) K51 A, 51 B.
2nd row: P51 B, 51 A.
Rep last 2 rows twice more. Now cont in patt from chart as foll:
1st row: K4 A, k across 94 sts of 1st row of chart reading from right to left, k4 B.
2nd row: P4 B, p across 94 sts of 2nd row of chart reading from left to right, p4 A. Cont in st st and patt from chart as set until 116 rows have been completed.
Next row: K51 D, 51 C.
Next row: P51 C, 51 D.
Rep last 2 rows twice more. Cast/bind off in colour patt.

BACK:

First piece: (Lower half)

With B, cast on 51 sts, then on to same needle cast on another 51 sts with A. 102 sts. Twisting yarns tog on WS of work when changing colour to avoid a hole forming, cont as foll:

1st row: (RS) K51 A, 51 B.

2nd row: P51 B, 51 A.

Rep last 2 rows to form st st until piece measures 22cm (8½in) from beg, ending with a p row.

Button band:

Cont in colours as set, work in moss/seed st as foll:

Next row: (K1, p1) to end.

Next row: (P1, k1) to end.

Rep last 2 rows 3 times more. Cast/bind off in moss/seed st.

Second piece: (Top half)

With 4mm (no. 8/US 6) needles and C, cast on 51 sts, then on to same needle cast on another 51 sts with D. 102 sts. Twisting yarns tog on WS of work when changing colour to avoid a hole forming, cont as foll:

1st row: (RS) K51 D, 51 C.

2nd row: P51 C, 51 D.

Rep last 2 rows to form st st until piece measures 22cm (8½in) from beg, ending with a p row.

Buttonhole band:

Cont in colours as set, work in moss/seed st as foll:

Next row: (K1, p1) to end.

Next row: (P1, k1) to end.

Next row: (K1, p1) to end.

Next row: Moss/seed st 11, (yo, k2tog, moss/seed st 24) 3 times, yo, k2tog, moss/seed st 11.

Work 4 more rows in moss/seed st. Cast/bind off in moss/seed st.

 # Making up

Carefully sew in all ends. Place cushion/pillow fronts WS down and position backs on top, with RS facing and overlapping button band over buttonhole band in centre. Sew tog all around outer edge. Turn cover RS out. Sew on buttons. Insert cushion pad/pillow form and button closed.

Flower cushion/pillow key:

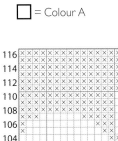 = Colour A   X = Colour C   — = Colour B   O = Colour D

Cape-style poncho

This easy-to-wear cape is perfect for slipping over your shoulders on chilly days.

In super-soft Aran (fisherman) yarn, this chic cape with its fold-back collar is self-striped in bands of simple stitches.

GETTING STARTED

Basic stitches and easy shaping make this an ideal project for beginners

Size:

To fit extra small/small[medium/large]

140[162]cm/55[63¾]in

53[58]cm/20¾[23]in

Figures in square brackets [ ] refer to the larger size; where there is only one set of figures, it applies to both sizes

How much yarn:

10[12] x 50g (2oz) balls of Sirdar Sublime Cashmere Merino Silk Aran, approx 86m (94 yards) per ball

Needles:

Pair of 5mm (no. 6/US 8) knitting needles

Tension/gauge:

18 sts and 24 rows measure 10cm (4in) square over st st on 5mm (no. 6/US 8) needles

What you have to do:

Work in stocking/stockinette stitch. Work in garter stitch (every row knit). Increase to shape cape at centre front and centre back by making stitches. Pick up and knit stitches around neck to work collar.

The Yarn

Sirdar Sublime Cashmere Merino Silk Aran is an exquisite blend of 75% extra fine merino with 20% silk and 5% cashmere to form a yarn that is extremely soft. Created in Aran (fisherman) weight, this yarn is available in ten luxuriously subtle shades for irresistible, textured knits.

Abbreviations:

= alternate;
= beginning;
= centimetre(s);
= continue;
= follow(s)(ing);
= garter stitch
(every row knit);
= increase(ing);
= knit;
= make one stitch by
picking up strand lying
between needles and
working into back of it; =
pattern;
= right side;
= stitch(es);
= stocking/stockinette
stitch

Instructions

BACK:

Note: Work in one piece from neck down.
Cast on 52[62] sts.
1st row: (RS) K25[30], m1, k2, m1, k25[30].
Beg with a p row, cont in st st, m1 as before either side
of centre 2 sts on every foll alt row to 60[78] sts, then on
every foll 4th row to 76[96] sts, ending with a p row.
Cont in 32-row patt as foll:
K16 rows g st, then beg with a k row, work 16 rows st st,
AT THE SAME TIME inc 2 sts as before on every foll 4th
row to 126[146] sts.
Work 13 rows straight so completing 16 rows of g st.
Cast/bind off loosely.

FRONT:

Work as given for Back.

COLLAR:

Join one side seam using backstitch.
With RS of work facing, pick up and k104[124] sts evenly
along neck edge.
Work 17[19]cm/6¾[7½]in g st.
Cast/bind off loosely.

 # Making up

Join remaining side and collar seam, reversing seam for last
12[14]cm/4¾[5½]in on collar.

HOW TO
BACKSTITCH

Use backstitch to join the seams on this poncho, matching the stitches when you place the pieces together.

3 Insert the needle one knitted stitch back and bring it out one knitted stitch ahead. Pull the yarn through to tighten and form a stitch.

1 Place the pieces to be joined right sides together. Match the rows of knitting stitch for stitch, and pin in place.

4 Repeat this step as you continue along the seam, making one backstitch cover one knitted stitch. Secure and trim the end of the yarn.

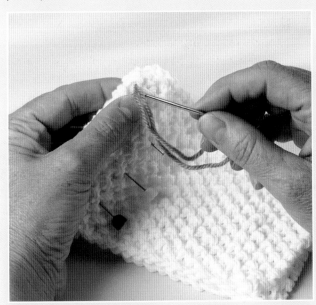

2 Thread a blunt-ended wool needle with yarn. Bring the needle through from the back to the front, one knitted stitch down from the starting edge.

Index

B
backstitch 127
basket, magazine 100
breakfast set 8

C
cakes 68
capes
   cape-style poncho 124
   soft cape 52
circular needles, how to use 55
crochet edging, how to work 87
cushions/pillows
   felted bobble cushion 48
   polka-dot cushion 24
   repeating flower cushion 120

E
egg cosies, breakfast set 8

F
fringe, how to make 39

G
gloves, all-stripe 40

H
hats
   Fair Isle bobble hat 60
   Peruvian-style hat 20
hot-water bottle cover, cuddly 72

I
intarsia 27

J
jacket, button-through 16

K
knitting needle case, striped 84

N
neck wraps
   checked neck wrap 112
   pompom neck wrap 12

P
pillows see cushions
placemat, breakfast set 8
pompoms, how to make 15, 47
ponchos
   cape-style poncho 124
   fringed poncho 36

S
scarves
   checked neck wrap 112
   fancy-fringed scarf 80
   pompom neck wrap 12
   skinny scarf 56
   skinny Fair Isle scarf 104
   striped scarf with pompoms 44
socks
   Fair Isle socks 76
   snazzy socks 32
stitch holder, how to use 91
sweater, boyfriend 88

T
tassel, how to make 23
tea cosies
   breakfast set 8
   dotty tea cosy 64
   funky Fair Isle tea cosy 116
tea-time treats 68
throws
   Aran throw 108
   featherweight throw 92
top, soft yoga 28

W
wrap, checkered 96

Y
yoga top, soft 28

Acknowledgements

Managing Editor: Clare Churly
Editors: Jane Ellis and Sarah Hoggett
Senior Art Editor: Juliette Norsworthy
Designer: Janis Utton
Assistant Production Manager: Caroline Alberti